Why Didn't They Tell Me?

99 Shameless Success Secrets They Don't Teach You At Eton, Harrow Or Even The Classiest Comprehensive!

By John Harrison

Published by
Streetwise Publications Ltd.®

Why Didn't They Tell Me?

99 Shameless Success Secrets They Don't Teach You At Eton, Harrow Or Even The Classiest Comprehensive!

First published in Great Britain by

Streetwise Publications Ltd.®
Eden House
Genesis Park
Sheffield Road
Rotherham
South Yorkshire S60 1DX
Tel: 01709 820033 Fax: 01709 360611
www.streetwisepublications.co.uk

A catalogue record for this book is available from the British Library.

ISBN: 978-0-9572059-0-1

INDEX

Foreword

Mark Twain remarked:

"When I was 14, I thought my father was an idiot.
Then when I became 21, I couldn't understand how
he'd learnt so much in just 7 years"

It's just amazing how simple it is to be successful in life, regardless of our definition of that emotive word 'success'. Success can be that mansion atop the hill, the shiny Ferrari or two in the garage, the bulging bank balance or the attractive partner draped on our arm. It can be a cure for plagues of body or mind, a life-changing breakthrough for those less fortunate - or anything else our hearts desire.

It matters not what definition we're striving to achieve – success is simple. Simple but NOT easy.

Here's why:

Mistakes! Yes – there are just so many mistakes you and I can make. If we took just ten minutes to start listing them, we'd quickly realise it would take more like ten years to complete the job! And there's the rub. There just isn't time to make all the mistakes to have a smooth passage through life.

So is there a solution?

Fortunately 'yes' – there is.

And it's a solution so well known you'd think it was a secret. Here it is: *"Listen to other people who've already travelled the road you wish to tread"* There it is – out in the open.

Even more fortunately for you – you have in the front of your eyes the definitive 'mistakes-avoiding' guidebook for life, your life and within its pages are the shortcuts to your ultimate goal – happiness in all its numerous guises and forms.

But – there's always a 'but' isn't there?

You have a major part to play in your success. Don't be seduced by the snake-oil salesmen peddling their 'just sit and think of success and it will appear'. Oh no! It won't. You have to use the other ingredient used by all successful people – action! Yes.

You **cannot** take responsibility for your results. There are just too many variables to take into consideration, which will affect the outcome. You CAN take responsibility for just two (and only two) items:

1. Your intent
2. Your actions.

Deepak Chopra said it mellifluously:

> *"Slip into the gap (the gap between your thoughts)*
> *with firm intent. Relinquish your attachment to the*
> *outcome and let the universe handle the details."*

Firm intent and appropriate action will see you achieve your desires.

John Harrison, by example, shows you the way. Be careful of taking advice from chip shop owners about being a successful retailer when there's no other chip shop within 50 miles of their success.

John has created success in a crowded 'street'. He's the real deal. He will be your best guide.

Let me leave you to your studies with these words:

> *There is a moment in every person's life*
> *When the awareness of their destiny*
> *Bursts like a bubble onto the surface of their conscious mind*
>
> *It is at that moment the weak avoid the realisation*
> *And busy themselves with mundane tasks*
>
> *It is also at that moment the strong awake*
> *And decide to change the world, their world for the better*
> *And by so doing secure for themselves*
> *Their rightful and valued place in the history of humankind*

Read on…

Peter Thomson
www.peterthomson.com

Introduction

Imagine that you woke up this morning to the sound of a Big Brother-style booming voice, announcing that you are about to go on an epic road journey. The trip will be several thousands of miles long, you'll start out alone and you'll be the one at the wheel. However, you don't get a choice of car and the one you'll be driving is waiting outside. You throw on some clothes, stagger downstairs, out of the front door and there it is on the drive.

You're not really happy with what you find. It's not the best-looking car you've ever seen and you wonder whether it is up to the journey. You're not happy with the bodywork and have a strong feeling that the engine will be hard to get started and keep running. What's more, you've only a vague notion of where you're supposed to be going and no real idea of how to get there. Your mind turns to the journey, and what it will take to make it a success.

You decide that the car is going to be important. Big Brother has already told you it's the only one you're going to get, so you quickly realise you'd better make the best of it. You want to make it look as good as possible (you figure out you may need passengers at some point and they're not going to want to get into a wreck) and you want to make sure it runs as well as possible for the whole journey. You wonder how you're going to do that.

Next you decide that you're going to need some kind of map. Big Brother has intimated that this journey isn't going to be straightforward or easy. You don't want to just rely on instinct and make it up as you go along. You need 'insider' information. Where are the shortcuts? Where are the dead ends? Where are the super-fast toll roads and what will it cost to use them? Where are the potholes and crumbling tracks that could scupper your journey altogether? How do you deal with the strange and varied driving habits of others along the way? Where are the best places to stop and explore as you go? Should you pick up passengers, and if so, who should they be? Where might it be dangerous to stop? And what's this whole journey about anyway?

You know nothing about any of this stuff, so what do you do? Well if you have even a single ounce of common sense, you seek out the help, support and guidance of those people who have done this before. You're not the first person to set off on this journey. The truth is that Big Brother has, at some point, rudely interrupted the slumber of just about every human being to ever walk the planet, and told him or her about the journey and the car. Most just rolled over and went back to sleep. It didn't excuse them the journey, but it certainly made it a lot less enjoyable, fulfilling and successful than it could, and should, have been.

The majority ended up getting stuck down blind alleys, delayed in traffic, weighed down by useless passengers, forced off the road by some lunatic in a juggernaut, or sat in a lay-by with smoke coming out of an engine they neither prepared nor maintained properly. All, long before their journey has reached its natural conclusion. Many just got lost and gave up. The really smart ones though, sought out and listened to what previous travellers had to say (yes, even the ones who'd got lost had important information to impart), used it as a basis for their trip and then built on that knowledge as they went along.

Why would you behave any differently on the most important journey of all?

I'm painfully aware that I face an uphill task here though. It was the author, Douglas Adams, who pointed out that: *"Human beings, are almost unique in their ability to learn from the experience of others, and also remarkable for their apparent disinclination to do so."* He might usefully have added that young human beings have the greatest disinclination of all. When you're young you know everything, so what the heck is there to learn?

When I started researching this whole subject, there was even more discouragement to be found. The innovative dancer, Isadora Duncan, in her autobiography *My Life,* offered the opinion that: *"What one has never experienced one will never understand in print",* while the US politician, Adlai Stevenson, mused: *"What a man knows at 50 which he didn't know at 20 is for the most part, incommunicable."* And yet I remain determined to communicate it, and make it understandable. Why? Because, quite frankly, I can think of few things that are more important.

You see, there comes a point in everyone's life when they stare wistfully into the distance, let out an involuntary audible sigh and utter these well-worn words for the first time: *"I wish I'd known… when I was younger. Why didn't somebody tell me?"* The bit that goes in the middle will vary of course, but it will be something important – perhaps something life transforming. It could be something that may have set their career on a stratospheric path, something that would have made them rich beyond their wildest dreams, something that would have made an important relationship work out, something that would have kept them safe or healthy. It could just be something that would have made them happier – perhaps something that would have stopped them wasting time, money and energy on things which didn't ultimately matter. Something that made them more 'successful' – whatever that might mean.

It may be the first time they've uttered those words, but it almost certainly won't be the last. Everyone has those 'I wish I'd known' moments after a certain age, and most of us have a lot of them. And it's with those moments in mind that this book was conceived and written. I want there to be a lot less of them – for you at least – and the best way I can think of achieving that is to give you a hefty dose of hindsight. It's the sort of thing that every young adult needs to know, but is woefully missing from most people's education – no matter how good the school they attended.

The Danish philosopher, Soren Kierkegaard, said: *"Life can only be understood backwards, but it must be lived forwards."* Those 'old folk', who wish that their younger selves were more knowledgeable, sigh because they have done precisely that. They've lived their lives forwards and now they understand it. If only they could go back and have a chat with themselves at sixteen, eighteen or twenty... twenty-five years of age even... life could turn out differently. Just one problem – they can't, and now many of their life chances and opportunities have either disappeared or, at least, diminished with the years. It's probably what the writer, Judith Stern, was talking about when she said: *"Experience is the comb that life brings you after you have lost your hair."*

Well guess what...you haven't lost your hair yet. Your mane is full and lustrous. Look on this book as the comb you're being given while you can still make full use of it. They say, somewhat ironically, that hindsight is a wonderful thing. When you're handed it in advance, it *is* a wonderful thing. It really is.

I said earlier that I face an uphill task here. Part of the reason for that, I've already highlighted – because it seems to be a human trait to be disinclined to learn from the experiences of others, and a trait particularly prevalent in the young. But there's another thing standing in your way of fully benefiting from what follows. I think the best way to explain it is to return to the hair and comb analogy.

When we're young we overestimate the amount of hair we have and how long it will last. The comb is left gathering dust in a drawer. *"There'll be plenty of time to use it later,"* we think. Without exception, as we grow older we realise that our hair is disappearing much faster than we could have imagined. And if we're not very careful, we will end up in the same position as the guy who handed us the comb all those years ago – bald and with a tool we can't really use.

Before you read another word, resolve to take action – and fast. If you take heed of only a fraction of the 'hindsight in advance' you're going to get here, your life will be immeasurably more fulfilling, rewarding and packed with achievements as a result. Samuel Butler, the composer and satirical author, said: *"Life is like playing a violin solo in public and learning the instruments as one goes on."* Look on this book as a series of 'behind closed doors' lessons. Take note and the chances of people covering their ears when you get on the public stage are greatly diminished.

Okay, enough about combs, violins and amusing analogies. What exactly are we going to talking about in the pages that follow?

In a nutshell, we're going to be talking about anything and everything that will make the journey that is your life, wealthier, healthier, happier and more fulfilling. To that end we'll be delving into money, careers, health and fitness, business and relationships. All viewed from the position of hindsight.

Not everything you read here will make sense to you right away. There will be things that you're not ready for yet. You can come back to those later. Just stick with it and apply what makes sense to you today. Taking on board just a handful of the ninety-nine secrets here can have a dramatic effect on how your life pans out.

The newspaper columnist, Miles Kington, said: *"Knowledge is knowing the tomato is a fruit, wisdom is not putting it in your fruit salad."* Most of us in our teens and early twenties have our heads stuffed with knowledge, but are woefully short on experience and wisdom. Is it any wonder that we wind up making some big mistakes? Some of these mistakes can take us so far off-track that it's hard to find a way back. There's no reason at all why that should happen to you. But you do have to be open to some ideas that will probably feel quite alien to you at the moment, and most important of all – you must take action.

In closing this brief introduction, I want to make something very clear. This book is totally centred on you, and helping you make the most of your life journey. There is no moral agenda; no attempt to shape changes that make for a better society or to turn you into a more valuable employee, employer, friend, son, daughter or anything else. The changes we're talking about here are to enhance *your* life, not someone else's. Rather conveniently though, it's almost impossible to do one without the other. When you transform your own life, you invariably transform the lives of those around you. That isn't our primary goal here, but it's a nice spin-off.

So help me prove Douglas Adams, Isadora Duncan and Adlai Stevenson wrong and grab this message with both hands. It can be communicated, it is understandable and you have it within you to learn based on the experience of others. Not only learn from it but act on what you've learned. What follows is the condensed experience of your predecessors. It's the stuff they know would transform their lives if they were given another go at it. They won't get that second chance of course, but you now have the opportunity to build on what they learned rather than starting from scratch. It would be, after all, rather foolish to pass up an opportunity like that?

Let the preparation for the journey begin!

You Have To Make It Happen.

The adjective that sums up many people's lives, when they are left to their own devices, is 'drifting'. They drift through school into a college or University course and then on into a job. Little or no thought is given to any of it. It's a course; it's a job. You're lucky to have either. It will do.

At the end of each day they drift home, eat some junk food, watch some junk TV and catch up with the latest junk gossip online. Sooner or later they will drift ever deeper into a relationship with someone with no real consideration for whether this person is right for them, and before they've had time to think about it (not that they would do anyway) they've drifted into parenthood, marriage or both.

Pretty soon, it's hard to tell one day from another, and one week imperceptibly blends into the next. Eventually longer periods also blend seamlessly into each other, with the only discernible difference between one year and the next being the size of their gut, the destination of their fortnight in the sun and the location of the office Christmas party.

Any changes they do make are purely reactive. They make no attempt to plan, create or actively advance. And before they know it, they're stuck in a rut with sides they can't see over the top of – approaching middle age and wondering where the hell their life went.

Think I'm over-dramatising? I've hardly started. And unless you make a firm commitment to take control of your own life and your destiny right now, this will happen to you too. Jim Rohn, the motivational speaker and writer, highlighted the problem very well. *"If you don't design your own life plan, chances are you'll fall into someone else's plan. And guess what they have planned for you? Not much."* By drifting, you make yourself cannon fodder – ripe for sacrifice in the pursuit of other people's plans.

To escape that fate, you have to take positive, proactive action now. You have to think, you have to plan and you have to take action. Nobody can, or will, do it for you. Nor will it happen by accident or magic. Drifting is an inevitable precursor to disappointment and failure. Whatever you want, it's up to you to take action to make it happen.

It's Later Than You Think.

You may not realise it yet, but the weeks, months and years will very soon start whizzing by at a rate you find hard to comprehend. If you've got things you want to do (and who of us hasn't?) it's never too early to get started.

You may not recognise the name Lenny McLean. In the 1970s and early 1980s he was 'king' of the unlicensed boxing ring. When he wasn't fighting men in the ring he was fighting them outside it as a bare-knuckle fighter, minder, debt collector and doorman – the sort of character for whom the word 'colourful' was invented! In his later years McLean moved into TV and films in small supporting roles, and his last appearance was in the hit film *Lock, Stock and Two Smoking Barrels*. I say last appearance, because while making the film he was diagnosed with terminal cancer and died soon after.

Now, up until being issued with a 'death sentence', McLean had always relied on his physical attributes and presence to make a living. He realised that this avenue was no longer open to him, and not only that, but decades of hitting and being hit had done little to benefit him financially. In short, he was effectively broke, and he knew that when he died his wife would have nothing. It dawned on McLean that the value in what he'd been doing for the last 30-odd years was not in the work he'd done, but in the story he could tell. And so he decided to write his autobiography. It was entitled *The Guv'nor* – McLean's nickname in the boxing ring.

When the book was published, it was an immediate hit and remained firmly placed in the Top Ten Bestsellers list for at least two years. I wouldn't be at all surprised if the autobiography ultimately earned far more than McLean made from his other activities throughout his entire career.

Sadly, he isn't around to benefit – and that's the point. This book could have been written at any time and McLean would have been able to enjoy the benefits, but it took something catastrophic to shift him out of his comfort zone and into a new, better and more lucrative course of action. In reality, most of us are like this. We have ambitions, we think there's probably a better way, we suspect there's more out there for us, but our current life isn't so bad. And so inertia gets in the way and stops us from taking the actions necessary to move on.

Yes, we want more but before we get it we have to do something. We have to take action. And that's the difficult bit. That's why we wait – to be made redundant… for an ailing business to finally collapse… for a milestone birthday… for New Year's Eve… to become ill or disabled… whatever – before finally doing something positive.

If we're fortunate and it's not too late, everything works out well, our new path is successful and we go from strength to strength. But why wait to be forced into a corner, or for some false and meaningless future date before doing it? After all, we can never get that wasted time back – the time between being able to do it and actually doing so. I think, the writer, Mark Twain, summed it up perfectly when he said: *"Twenty years from now, you'll be more disappointed by the things you didn't do than the ones you did do. So throw off the bowlines. Sail away from the safe harbour. Catch the trade winds in your sails. Explore, dream, discover."*

It's a great quote, and so true. Speak to most people in the later years of their lives and you will rarely hear talk of things that they wish they hadn't done; but plenty of talk about opportunities which have now passed, and which should have been seized upon at the time.

Three of the saddest words to start any sentence are: *"If only I'd..."* How many times have you heard them? You really don't want to be the one using them in twenty years' time.

Can you imagine anyone lying on his or her deathbed, with a saddened look in their eyes, and saying: *"I wish I'd spent a bit more time in that dead-end job"*? Neither can I. But the truth is that millions lie there wishing that they'd chased their dream; that they'd taken that chance...

Don't be one of them.

This Is As Good As It Gets.

How do you feel about the following statements?

*"The trade of advertising is now so near perfection that
it is not easy to propose any improvement."*

"Everything that can be invented has been invented."

I think most of us would at least see some truth there. Advertising is very sophisticated now, even compared to 15 or 20 years ago. Surely we must be close to the limit of what can be done.

And the same could be said of invention and innovation. Over the past 100 years we've invented practically everything man ever dreamed of, and a great deal more besides. In recent years the computer and the digital revolution seem to have completed the picture. It certainly seems like there's little of any consequence left to be invented.

If you find yourself nodding in agreement with any of the above, consider the following... The writer, Samuel Johnson, made the first statement, highlighting the perfection of the advertising business, in 1759 – over 250 years ago. The second statement, bemoaning the downfall of invention, was made by Charles Duell, US Patent Office Commissioner in 1899 – over 100 years ago. In fact, his disillusionment caused him to resign from his job. Still, I'm sure he didn't miss much.

Here's the point. Pick any time in history and you will find that people felt that previous generations had it easier, that the opportunities were better and more plentiful, that it was so much more simple to make your mark in the world. If only we could have been around then. We'd have really made a go of it! We have a word for this. We call it nostalgia. Fact is, when we look back at past opportunities we do so with the benefit of hindsight. When we're assessing the current openings available to us we have to do so using foresight. And that's considerably less reliable!

We can all look back a comparatively short time and say how much easier it would have been back then to prosper in computers, software, mobile phones or a host of other markets that were in their infancy at the time. And we may well be right. But the people getting out there and actually doing it at the time didn't really know that for sure. It's only hindsight that adds the certainty. Foresight created the profit.

Here in the 21st Century, you can be sure that the new opportunities available, and the avenues for improving existing opportunities, are at least as plentiful as at any time in history. They're just not as obvious to you because you don't have the benefit of hindsight to guide you.

Don't fall into the nostalgia trap. In ten years' time, these will be the *"good old days"* when 'getting on' was as easy as falling off a log. By then, of course, things won't be nearly so easy, and opportunities won't be nearly as plentiful. Except, of course, they will. Remember, becoming a success in whatever you want to do is as easy as it's ever going to get. There's absolutely no logical reason for looking back, or delaying making a start for a moment longer.

The World Is Awash With Cheats.

When my daughter was eight she moved from one primary school to another. The new place was completely different. Educational standards were much higher and structure and discipline were right at the top of the list of priorities. Everybody was expected to dress and behave correctly and treat each other with respect. I'd have hated it, but she absolutely loves the place.

A few days after starting she came in from school, excited about the afternoon they'd just spent preparing and practising for sports day the following week. *"It's so much better than at the other place,"* she said, *"It's a lot stricter… there's no thumbs on eggs!"*

I wasn't sure whether this was a good or bad thing because I know one thing for sure – out in the real world, she's almost certain to come up against people with thumbs planted firmly on eggs. It doesn't matter what she wants to do, she'll inevitably come up against people who are bending or breaking the rules in order to win. And that's the same for you. So how should you react?

Well the universal default solution seems to be to whine and whinge about the injustice and unfairness of it. This is usually accompanied by feelings of anger and stress. So you'll moan and groan and let off a few expletives. You'll use the word unfair a lot. But does that do any good? Of course it doesn't, and it can only have a damaging effect on your health if you allow yourself to be affected like that. So what CAN you do?

Well you could complain to the 'referee'. Depending on the field you're operating in, and the seriousness of the thumb-on-egg transgression, that referee could be the police, a court, a trade association, a regulatory body, an ombudsman or some other higher authority. There may be times when that's a sensible course of action, but most of the time, it won't be.

Why? Because it will be time-consuming, expensive and will divert you from your primary goals. When you're eight years old and at school, telling the teacher is a viable solution. It's quick, cost-free and usually effective. In the real world, it's slow, expensive and the outcome is uncertain. Over the years, I've had cause to appeal to the 'referee' on a number of occasions, and although I've almost always won, it's rarely felt like it.

So is there an alternative? Actually there are three…

You can stick your own thumb on the egg. Pretty simple this one. If you can't beat 'em, you decide to join 'em. There are, however, two key considerations here – your moral position and the possible consequences of sliding your thumb over that egg. If your moral position is such that any egg holding is completely out of the question, then the consequences are largely irrelevant. This option just isn't for you. You have to live with yourself and you have to sleep soundly at night.

But if you find yourself wavering a little, you need to assess the possible consequences, the potential rewards, and whether one justifies the other. It's impossible to generalise here because in one situation you may be risking jail for a few hundred pounds and in another you may be risking a mild rebuke from a trade association for a million. In reality, your situation will fall somewhere between the two, and the course of action you choose will be a very personal decision.

Your second option is to just accept it. So you find out as much as you can about the way these people work, counteract it where you can, and don't worry about the places where you can't. You work within your own moral code and framework at all times, and don't concern yourself with people who operate within a different framework. If you want to continue in your field, and aren't comfortable stretching the boundaries, then this is the only sensible long-term option. The main shift you need to make is a psychological one, and I can't pretend it's easy. Simple – yes. Easy – no. Because like a drug-free athlete in the Olympic Games, you have to accept that the price of your stance is that you're not going to win, and lesser performers will beat you.

Your final option is to get out of the race altogether. You're in a race. Your competitors are cheating. You don't like it. You may decide to go and compete in another race where the competitors aren't so nasty. Now this may be an option if you happen to have found yourself in the dirtiest race in town, but you need to be sure of that first. The harsh truth is that you may find yourself jumping from the frying pan into the fire. As any hardened eight-year-old egg-and-spoon race contestant will tell you, you often can't see the thumbs on eggs until you're in the race and running alongside.

I can't and won't tell you what you should do. All I can do is to alert you to the undeniable fact that whatever race you get involved in in life, a number of your competitors will be keeping their egg in place with something other than skill and ability. I'm not going to say you should bend the rules; call in the referee; just accept it or get out of the game altogether. But I am going to tell you not to whinge and whine about how unfair it all is, because it won't change a damned thing. Nobody ever said it was fair. The only question is what are you going to do about it?

There's one more solution I haven't told you about yet. You see, not all egg-and-spoon-race cheats are as obvious as to put their thumbs on their eggs. The really canny ones are a little cleverer than that and use a small piece of Blu Tack to attach the egg to the spoon. It's almost as effective, but totally undetectable to either the referee or fellow competitors – even when they're running alongside.

If I were looking to secure an unfair advantage, I'd choose the Blu Tack on the spoon every time. I'll leave you to ponder where the Blu Tack opportunities might be in your life.

Your Time Is Now.

When you're young it's very easy to bemoan your lack of experience and resources, but you currently sit on some huge untapped resources that older people can't hope to match.

Here's a little test for you…

Name a song written by Paul McCartney. Too easy? Okay, how about a song written by David Bowie. I'm not really testing you am I? Here's the last one – name a song written by Elton John.

Anyone with an average interest in popular music would fairly easily be able to name at least one song by each songwriter, and in most cases, be able to name quite a few. But now I'm going to make that question a bit harder by adding five words – so hard in fact, that I suspect that not one in a 100 people could answer it. Here are those five extra words… *"In the last ten years."*

You see, each of those songwriters is still actively writing songs, and yet their 'best' work – the work for which they will be remembered long after they are dead – was condensed into a short 'hot' period early in their career. Despite being older and (in theory) more experienced, their later work somehow hasn't carried the same resonance as that which they created in the early days.

Now I haven't picked these songwriters out because they are exceptions. Choose any popular songwriter from the last 40 years and you'll find the same thing – a comparatively short 'hot' period early in their careers followed by an awful lot of plodding… Michael Jackson, Noel Gallagher, George Michael – all the same. As I write this, Adele is going through a similar 'hot' period. So what's going on?

Everyone has an untapped source of creativity lurking just below the surface. It's a hidden store of wonderful ideas and inspiration that lies there, waiting to be released. The scale of this untapped source will vary from person to person of course, (we don't all have a McCartney-sized well of musical ideas in there for example) but what we have, isn't unlimited. Once the creative flow has started, ideas flood out very quickly, but eventually the flow will diminish, as will the quality of those ideas. In the case of songwriters, they come to rely on perspiration rather than inspiration after that – on what they know and have learned, rather than what flows from within. But it's never the same.

It appears that a similar process takes place, no matter what the purpose of your creativity – whether that is art, literature, music or something more mundane like a business or career progression. When you embark on a business or money-making venture for the first time for example, the ideas for products, advertising and promotions you come up with in the early days will be amongst the most creative you ever have, because they will come from within. They will be the equivalent of McCartney's *Yesterday* – not one of the countless pop songs he's penned in the last 25 years or so.

And that's why, contrary to what you might think, you start with a massive advantage over the established players in any field requiring creativity – an advantage that helps counteract some of the experiences and advantages which older people have. Your well of ideas is both untapped and full.

This will be a golden period for you, and the really good news is that you have total exclusivity over it. Your combination of skills, experience, ability, personality and innate talent is unique. And the ideas and inspirations that spring from that combination will be unique too.

Life Isn't Fair. Get Over it!

Here's something you need to accept and work with, very quickly. We first hear kids in the playground complaining that *"it's not fair"*, and, if it goes unchecked, they're still saying the same thing when they're drawing their pension. It's pointless and self-defeating.

Life isn't fair. Nobody ever said that it was. People are born with differing natural attributes and some of these attributes have an impact on what we see as fairness. Sometimes, people will be given favourable treatment because of these attributes, which isn't warranted. Good-looking people, for example, are often favoured in situations where looks don't really matter. Quiet, thoughtful and sensible people are often passed over in favour of the charismatic, dogmatic and wayward. The kind and virtuous often receive no reward, while calculation and deceit goes unpunished. The talented, hard-working and able often lose out to those with the 'right connections'. Fairness just doesn't come into any of it.

Why is this important? Because many go through life waiting for things to become fair and recoiling from situations where they are not. If you do this, you will become severely disenchanted and miss out on a lot of opportunities. Life will never be fair. If you're on the positive side of unfairness, don't feel guilty. Capitalise on it. If you're on the negative side, don't moan or give up. Recognise what's happening and take action. Unfairness can usually be overcome by effort and application. Those who are unfairly favoured have a tendency towards complacency that makes them easier to prevail over than you might think.

You Have To Come First.

I have a friend who's mad about cars, but he never keeps one for longer than about six months. And what's more, when he buys his cars, he knows he won't be keeping them for a long time. So he doesn't really look after them. Servicing doesn't get done, cleaning is never more than a quick run through the car wash, and he isn't averse to giving them a fair amount of 'stick'. You see he knows that any ill effects from this rough treatment will be someone else's problem, because he'll just trade in – and move on.

I have another friend who isn't crazy about work, but he does tend to keep his jobs for about the same length of time as my first friend keeps his cars. Not that he gets the sack; it's just that he gets bored very quickly. He knows from the very first day on a job that his stay will be short-lived, and because he knows that, his commitment is less than 100%. He does just enough to get by. Corners are cut, liberties are taken and he never goes that extra inch (let alone that extra mile) to impress the people he's working for to progress in the organisation. He knows that long before the chickens come home to roost, he'll have resigned and moved on.

These friends are cavalier with their car and their job because they know they have an escape route – an easy way to avoid the nasty consequences of their actions. What happens in the long run in these specific situations doesn't really matter to them. Now you might not like what they do… and you certainly won't if you're the next poor person to step into that particular car or job… but you have to admit that there's a certain logic to it. The trade-in and resignation offer a pre-planned escape… one that makes doing 'the right thing', a matter of choice rather than necessity. But how do you explain the behaviour of people who live their whole life the same way… as if they will soon be able to resign from it, or trade it in for a new one?

You see the hard truth is that you can't resign from yourself – nor can you trade yourself in. You have no choice but to persevere with what you've got and work with it. You're stuck with you!

In automotive terms, you are the only car you're ever going to have. In career terms you're the only employer you'll ever work for. There are no 'dealers' where you can trade in your life, when your personal neglect gets the outcome it deserves. And as far as I know, there's only one guaranteed resignation option in life, but it's not one that results in you finding another position. (Not above ground at least!) This is so fundamentally important, it underpins and supports just about everything you do in life.

Imagine you have a company, and you are allowed just one employee. Not only is he your only employee – he's also the only employee you can ever have. You can't replace him and he can't leave. The success or failure of your entire enterprise rests with him. So how are you going to treat him?

Are you going to let him vegetate on a sofa eating junk food and smoking Player's Full Strength while watching Sky Sports – or are you going to encourage him in the direction of healthy eating, cleaner living and regular exercise? Are you going to leave him to pick up the job by trial and error, or are you going to invest in the best possible training so that he can operate at the absolute limits of his ability? Are you going to leave him to his own devices, or are you going to continually monitor and analyse his performance – identifying any weaknesses and taking steps to put them right? Are you going to assume that once he's been trained, you can forget about him, or are you going to take the view that the world is in a continual state of change and he needs to be regularly updated and trained on new ideas and developments? If he becomes unhappy or dissatisfied, are you going to conclude that there's nothing you can do about it, or are you going to take the time to 'nail down' the problem, and come up with a solution for him?

Think very carefully before you answer, because you are that employee and the enterprise is your life. When you look at it like that, wouldn't it be astounding if you didn't invest the maximum time, money and effort in developing and maintaining yourself so that you are the best you can possibly be?

You Have To Play The Hand You've Been Dealt.

Every year the World Series of Poker is held in Las Vegas – the world championship of the game. It's a game with, seemingly, a large element of chance attached. The players can, after all, only play with the cards they're given.

In the long term, the law of averages dictates that luck will be pretty evenly distributed amongst the players. You would therefore expect that the outcome of tournaments to fluctuate widely depending on the varying fortunes of those taking part. That's not what happens. Although results do vary, the same good players perform consistently well, irrespective of the cards they're dealt. And it's the same in life.

It's all too easy to complain about the cards you've been dealt and use that as an excuse for failure. The top players accept the cards they're given – there's nothing you can do about that –and then work out how best to use them to get the results they're after. Even when people are dealt great cards, it's all too easy to waste them.

At the risk of boring anyone not interested in football, it does provide us with an excellent example, showing why the 'cards' you're dealt in life are less important than how they are used.

There can be few footballers dealt a better hand than George Best. Most experts agree that he was one of the most naturally gifted players of all time. And yet by the age of 26, when he should have been at his best, he virtually disappeared from the game, as did his opportunity to become the richest and most successful player of his generation. Few have achieved so little with so much.

At the same time as Best was ending his career, Kevin Keegan was just starting his. He was too small, too thin, and by his own admission, lacked great natural footballing ability. It would have been all too easy for him to give in to the hand he'd been dealt and accept that he would never be a top player because he didn't have Best's ability. But through hard work and determination he rose to become captain of his country and to win practically every honour in the game, making a not inconsiderable fortune for himself in the process.

Hard work and determination are not the only ways to overcome a terrible hand. For the moment, I'm going to stick with my football analogy…

A player who few would place in the 'gifted' category is Vinnie Jones. In fact, few would place him in their pub first team if footballing skill were the sole criteria! And yet he consistently played in the top division, represented his country and made a lot of money in the process. There are literally thousands of 'Vinnie Joneses' out there, but few get to play professionally at all. Certainly hard work and determination played a part, but so did a commitment to playing the game on his own terms.

If Jones had tried to play the game like George Best, he wouldn't have lasted five minutes. What he had to do was establish his strengths and play to them. He concentrated on what he could do, not what he couldn't. Occasionally that may have meant bending some of the rules, but that's what ordinary players have to do sometimes to stay in the game.

Jones was to prove that what he achieved in football was no fluke. He later used the same flare for playing his hand to the maximum in a completely separate field – one to which he would seem equally ill-suited. 'Vinnie Jones the footballer' became 'Vinnie Jones the Hollywood film star'. Just as he didn't try to emulate Best on the football field, he didn't try to emulate Sir John Gielgud, Sir Ian McKellen or even Tom Cruise on screen. But he did play the hand he had been dealt to great effect.

It doesn't take a massive leap of logic to see that there's a message here for anyone aiming for a business or personal goal. You may not have been dealt the hand of a George Best, or a Lionel Messi but that is no barrier to success. Learn to play your hand well, and you can usually beat most of those dealt a better one.

The key to success is accepting your hand (you won't get another one!) and adapting to it where necessary. Certainly it may involve hard work, and you may have to make the rules work for you, rather than the other way round. But the end result when you achieve it will be all the more rewarding.

Successful People Are Plonkers Too.

An email from a reader of my online newsletter gave me cause to think consciously about something that up until then had been active on a sub-conscious level. Here's what he said:

> *"I think the fact you present your public face, and also in your newsletter you outline the fact that you are also human and aren't afraid to present your vulnerable side when appropriate, helps."*

I think what he meant – but was perhaps too polite to say – is that I'm prepared to let everyone know what a plonker I really am. And when I think about it, he's right. Let me tell you why…

When I was growing up, and in the period before I started to have some business and financial success, I didn't know any millionaires. I didn't even know anyone you could describe as wealthy. Everyone I knew was just like me – or not far from it. The richest person I knew ran the local greengrocers. That gives you some idea of what I'm talking about.

Because I didn't actually know anyone who had accumulated wealth, the rich were a bit of a mystery to me. And there's not a great deal of difference (both literally and linguistically) between mystery and mystique. The information and impressions I had came from newspapers, glossy magazines and TV. And when presented in these selective media outlets, you don't really get a true or accurate picture. Everyone who'd achieved financial success seemed impossibly sophisticated or charismatic or glamorous or educated or skilled or… or… something other than what I was.

And it was all a bit off-putting and demotivating. When you aspire to something, the first stage is to believe it's possible. If you see other people who've already done it – people who share your background, imperfections and insecurities – then that's very powerful in persuading you that you can do it too. If you see people with whom you have little in common, it makes it seem all the harder and more distant.

Once I started to achieve some success, and got to meet others who'd done the same, I realised that, like me, there was nothing intrinsically special or unusual about them. The difference was in what they'd done… how they'd played the cards they'd been dealt… rather than what they were. And so when I got the opportunity to communicate with people who were looking to move forward with their lives, it just seemed natural that I would present things as they are, rather than perpetuating myth and mystique. If you want to give people the best chance of following in your footsteps, why would you do any other?

The wealthy and successful are just like you. They started out with the same insecurities, doubts and hang-ups that you have today. They have the same stupid thoughts and, out of the public gaze, are just as capable of making complete pillocks of themselves as anyone else. They are made of no better or worse stuff than you and, as such, there are no genuine barriers to you joining them.

Everyone Gets Dumped On – Rejoice!

Crap happens to me, it happens to you… and it happens to Bill Gates.

Back in the days when I was struggling, I used to think that wealthy and successful people led some kind of utopian existence. They made their way in the world by having fortune shine down upon them and then used their money to ward off all the tedious and nasty things that happen to ordinary folk. Well now I know it's not like that. Success doesn't depend on not having crap things happen to you. It depends on dealing with crap when it happens.

Let me put that a bit more politely. To be successful you have to deal effectively with the adversity that impacts everyone. Once you become successful, you'll still have to deal with adversity. If you think success will make you immune to adversity – you're wrong. It won't.

We all get pretty much the same amount of luck in our lives. Oh sure, you go through times where nothing seems to go right. Everybody does. But over the long haul… whether it's in your career, business or personal life… everyone gets broadly the same amount of luck. It's what you do with it that matters.

But here's an interesting thing. When something does go wrong – when it seems like Lady Luck is just having a laugh – that event will almost certainly contain within it, the seeds of something positive. You just need to look for it. If you take just one thing from this book, make it a commitment to seek out the positive seeds in each piece of adversity you encounter. They're there. I can promise you that.

In my business, every single time I've had a setback, when something hasn't worked as well as it should, or a deal or project has fallen through, it has caused me to seek out a solution or replacement project that has led to even better things. Here's just one example…

When we first started out in the direct response business, we needed to rent mailing lists. I approached the biggest supplier of the type of lists we wanted at the time, but they refused to deal with us. I don't know whether they were afraid of the competition or thought we were small fry wasting their time (probably the latter). Anyway, I needed a solution.

So I found a broker who sourced for us some fantastic lists that really formed the bedrock of the business we have today. About a year later, the original company I'd approached decided we were now worth dealing with, and let us use their lists.

Guess what? Their lists were terrible! If they'd let us have them 12 months earlier, I'd have probably concluded that the direct response business wasn't for me and given up.

The setback… the piece of bad luck… was a blessing in disguise.

What I'm trying to get over to you is this – success of any type has nothing to do with luck. Over the long haul, and aside from some very extreme cases for which you do NOT qualify, there's no such thing as bad luck. There is just stuff that happens to you… the same stuff that happens to everyone else at some point in their lives. It's what you do that matters.

Some people learn, look for the positive angle and move on. Others give up. Those who give up are the ones who believe they're 'just unlucky' and it's their fate to fail. *"Why beat yourself up,"* they might say, *"if the stars/gods/fates are against you?"*

Those who move forward are the people who know that luck has absolutely nothing to do with it – that their success or failure is completely, utterly and exclusively, down to them. How can you give in when there's nobody or nothing else to blame?

You Get To Pick Your Own Role, So Choose Well.

One of the most widely known quotations from Shakespeare's play *As You Like It* is: *"All the world's a stage and all the men and women merely players."* Perhaps you've not given it much thought; I know I hadn't until I came across a couple of other things.

The first was a book by Derren Brown called *Tricks of The Mind*. In one chapter, Brown discusses the subject of developing and displaying confidence. Now if you've ever seen Brown perform, I think you'll agree that he comes across as being supremely confident. And yet it wasn't always like that, and indeed isn't necessarily like that today.

You see, in his early life, Brown suffered from the same doubts and insecurities as most of us. So what made the difference? Well he discovered something very simple, and yet extraordinarily powerful – in order to become confident, you firstly have to act confident. Once you start to act in a confident manner, others begin to treat you as confident, and guess what? You become confident because of the way other people are now treating you. It becomes a self-fulfilling prophecy.

The second thing that happened concerned one of the actors who features in a film I'd been working on. Part of 'the deal' when you star in a film is that you're expected to help promote it. Now acting and promotion are two completely different things, which is why the cast of this film were booked in for a training session on how to present themselves in interviews. Some of the cast were 'naturals', but one guy (I won't say who to save his blushes) just wasn't comfortable with this sort of attention. Whilst he comes to life on screen, in private he's pretty quiet and unassuming. Perfectly fine qualities in a human being, but not so great when you're trying to excite and enthuse people about the film you've just made.

The lady running the course had seen all this before and knew exactly what to do. Instead of giving him a list of specific instructions, which she knew he'd probably forget anyway, she gave him just one instruction... *"Just imagine it's a part, and you're playing a successful movie star!"*

As soon as he twigged this... that he wasn't being himself in these interviews he was simply playing a part, just as he did every day of his working life, the transition was near-instantaneous. He acted like a movie star, so people started to treat and react to him as though he was a movie star. You know what happens next... he'll start to feel like a movie star, and that will affect how he behaves naturally. But like Derren Brown, he had to consciously choose the role before it became part of him.

Is there an 'Aha!' moment there for you? I know there was one for me. The world is indeed a stage and we're all playing parts. The great news is that we get to choose the parts we play. Nobody else chooses those parts for us. If we play the part well, the world demands and dictates that we play it for life. But it works both ways. Choose a lousy part for yourself – and if you don't apply conscious effort and thought to this, you probably will – and that's the part the world will allocate to you too.

Once you realise that, you become what you present yourself as being, it's a tremendously enlightening and empowering moment, because you know that your fate and fortunes lay entirely in your own hands. But it can be a frightening moment too, because every excuse you ever had for not being where and what you want to be, is stripped away in an instant. And there's comfort to be had in excuses.

Fail To Prepare And You Prepare To Fail.

Two brothers supported the same football team. At the end of every game, the team captain picked up the match ball and kicked it into the crowd. Whoever caught the ball got to keep it. Both brothers badly wanted one of those balls.

The first brother turned up for every home game, sat in his usual seat, and watched as the ball was hoofed into the stand – most of the time at the opposite end of the ground. Once, the ball did come near him but he wasn't really paying attention, and someone, a few seats along, grabbed it. After every game he went home cursing his bad luck. The second brother did things differently.

For a full season, he carefully watched where the ball landed. He noted that 80% of the time the team captain kicked the ball into the South Stand, and that, more often than not, it landed between Rows 15 and 20. In the close season, he spent an hour every day kicking a football into the air and catching it. When he purchased a season ticket for the following season it was in Row 17 of the South Stand. When the players came off the field at the end of the first game, he kept his eyes on the team captain until he'd picked up the match ball and kicked it into the crowd.

Now let me ask you this – which of those two brothers do you think is the most likely to be 'lucky'?

If Shakespeare was right about the world being a stage and everyone being merely players, the need to prepare and rehearse seems obvious. And yet so few people do it. We stumble into important interviews, meetings and social interactions with only a vague idea of what we will say, how we will act or how other key players will act or react. Everything comes as a surprise and, as a result, we fail to make the most of the opportunities that are presented to us.

To fully capitalise on the opportunities life gives us, it's vital that we prepare and rehearse. This will mean different things to different people in varying situations, but preparation can take both mental and physical forms. Few opportunities arrive 'out of the blue', but even if they do, that doesn't mean you shouldn't rehearse. If you walked into a lift and the only other person there just happened to be the one person in the world who could make your dreams come true, you know exactly what you would say to them – don't you?

Time spent preparing and rehearsing is rarely wasted and is so often the difference between success and failure. Don't ever step onstage without knowing your lines. In the real world there are no 'prompts' to bail you out.

You Get What You Expect.
So Expect More!

Welcome to my psychiatrist's chair. Make yourself comfortable and ease right back because I want to take you back to your early childhood.

You were five years old and you saw a toy you really wanted. I mean you *really* wanted it, so you went to your parents, and asked if you could have the toy for your birthday. Did they say: *"yes, of course, no problem at all."* Chances are, they didn't. If they were like most parents, they said: *"wait and see."* If you pressed them, you probably got: *"Well, if you expect, you won't get!"*

Whether you got the toy or not, this sort of response was one you probably became accustomed to hearing over the years – no definite commitment, and always the warning not to expect too much.

Of course, there were perfectly good reasons for this. Your parents weren't sure whether they'd be able to get the toy for you. They'd be concerned that they couldn't afford it when the time came, or that the shops would be out of stock. It was all down to them, and their response reflected that. They didn't want to disappoint you; so there was always a warning to lower your expectations, not to expect too much, because unfulfilled expectation leads to abject disappointment in your average five-year-old child, and no parent wants that.

I'm sure you can see where I'm heading with this. Psychologists, personal development experts, and just about everyone else who has studied the human psyche and the factors determining success and failure, broadly agree on two important things:

1. What we learn in early childhood has a significant on-going effect on our thoughts and behaviour throughout our lives – unless we make a determined effort to re-programme and re-learn.

2. We get pretty much what we expect to get from life, but rarely more. Expectation always precedes acquisition.

So we have a situation where early childhood has created a general tendency towards low expectation. At the time it was appropriate – you had no control over the fulfilment, or otherwise, of your expectation. You'd be devastated if your expectation wasn't met. But all that's changed now. You've grown up. You have control, and what's more, you're big enough to take it on the chin if you fall short of what you expect.

Low expectations are completely at odds with achievement, financial or otherwise. Very little of any consequence is ever achieved without the expectation and belief that it can be done – except when it happens by sheer accident. Why?

Because we only take the actions necessary to achieve success when we expect a successful outcome. In any endeavour, there will be setbacks and low points. The only thing that gets us through these is the belief – the expectation – that we will ultimately succeed. If we don't believe and expect that we'll ultimately triumph, why the hell should we put ourselves through the pain and difficulty of pressing on through adversity?

Can you see how high expectation must always precede high achievement, and how your early conditioning might be holding you back from achieving your full potential now? It's definitely worth taking a little time to assess whether your expectations are as high as they should be, and whether they're being created and shaped by old and obsolete influences. What you discover may surprise you. And this doesn't just apply to achievement. Your expectations shape everything.

From time to time, I visit an online forum for people who have nothing better to do with their money than waste it on expensive cars. Just out of curiosity, you understand. Anyway, two of the topics, which repeatedly come up, are: *"When at a junction, which of your cars is least likely to be let out by other drivers?"* And: *"Which car is likely to get the most abuse from members of the public?"* Opinions always vary widely.

Some people say that you can sit there all day in a Ferrari, but be let out straightaway in an Aston Martin, while others swear the reverse is true. Someone else will say they've driven Porsches for years with no bother, but get hassle from all quarters in their Bentley, and then another Bentley owner will say this is nonsense. Then others say they get little courtesy and lots of hassle in any car that is out of the ordinary. But then there are people, like me, who say it doesn't make a blind bit of difference.

It's true. I've had more than my fair share of very nice cars over the years and I find that being let out at a junction while driving one is no more trouble than when driving a bog standard saloon. I've never experienced any animosity from people, and the only conversations I've had while driving something unusual, have been the result of genuine interest and curiosity. So how come people's experiences vary so greatly?

The answer has implications for just about everything we do. You see it's pretty clear that the cars are no different, and the public who are reacting to them are the same. The only thing that's changed is the driver. Each driver will have his own opinion on how people are going to react to his car, and this opinion will form the basis of his expectations.

If you drive your Ferrari believing that everyone is going to be hostile, then that's what you'll find. If you believe they're going to be interested and friendly, then you'll find that too. It's partly a result of how your expectation affects your behaviour, and partly your own perception of the reaction. If you expect to see hostility, that's what you will see. If you expect to see interest, then *that's* what you'll see.

I'm sure, like me, you know people who get into fights easily. And then you know others who go to the same environments, who never have so much as a crossed word. The former will always claim that it isn't their fault – that trouble just seems to follow them around. And it does, because that's what they expect.

If they go into the same environment expecting something else, then the vast majority of the time, 'something else' is what they'll get. Their demeanour and body language will be non-confrontational, drastically reducing the likelihood of causing offence, and their perception of the behaviour of others will be positively focused, eliminating the chances of imagined slights.

I can't over-emphasise how important expectations are. They almost totally shape our future reality (barring outrageous good or bad fortune). If you're hoping for success, but grimly expecting failure, you have little chance, if any. Your subconscious mind will find a way for you to fail, and your conscious mind will, in the most unlikely of places, recognise signals that it's time to give up.

When you expect success, every glimmer of hope is a clear sign that you're on the right track. When you expect failure, every tiny setback is confirmation that you should give up. You're going to get what you expect, so you might as well expect something good.

The Secret Of A Happy Life Is Four Words Long.

If your great great grandparents were resurrected tomorrow, they'd be stunned...

We travel where and when we choose at astonishing speed and at very little cost. Goods and services are in almost limitless supply and everything there is to see and know is practically there at the click of a computer mouse or via a smartphone screen.

Go back just four generations, and the poor were undernourished and thin. No longer. How would you explain to your great great grandfather that the 'poor' of today are usually the people who eat way too much? Take any wealth and well-being measurement you like... per capita income, car ownership, real spending power, health, home ownership and size... and the trend is always upward and always improving. Our wealth and prosperity, and the factors connected with them, just get better and better. Forget nostalgia about the good old days... if there's ever been a Golden Age, one where economic prosperity has created freedom, opportunity and the good things in life, it is right here and now. It's never been any better than this.

But if that's the case, let me ask you this – are you any happier than your parents were at your age... or your grandparents? You have good 'stuff' in your life, 'stuff' they could have never dreamed of. But unless you're very unusual, the answer will be *"no"* – you are not happier than the preceding generation.

Throughout the Western world something strange is happening. As prosperity grows, so does the incidence of depression. Experts calculate that depression is 10 times more prevalent than it was 50 years ago.

Psychologist after psychologist has come up with the same conclusion – people are less satisfied and less happy than at any time in recent history. And yet by any measure, they're more prosperous. Real happiness and fulfilment clearly can't be bought. And if you want confirmation of that, you need look no further than the average lottery winner.

Most people buy a lottery ticket with the expectation that if they 'win the big one', it will transform their life for the better... for all time. And yet research by Dr Nick Baylis of Cambridge University suggests that the average lottery winner's happiness quotient returns to its pre-win level within one year of the win. Acquisition of goods and services bring them no long-term improvement in happiness – just a short-term 'buzz', followed by a storage and 'looking after' headache! The new possessions give no pleasure – just hassle and worry. And then pain if they're taken away.

But I think it goes further than that, because many winners end up less happy than they were before. The money has robbed them of something very important... the belief that there is a simple solution to their personal happiness problem – a great pile of cash! Once they realise that the money has failed to do the 'trick' they feel lost. All hope of a simple solution easily purchased in the shape of a lottery ticket, is gone.

Now they're going to have to find the real key to happiness, but they haven't got a clue where to look. Maybe they should try the Jacuzzi.

I was talking to a friend at my local health club in the Jacuzzi. He'd just sold his business and was thinking about what to do next. Paul had enough money to retire on, but after a few weeks of inactivity, he was starting to get restless. Brendan, who quickly caught up with the conversation, joined us.

Now Brendan is quite well known locally. He's a boxing trainer who has successfully trained several British European and World champions, including Prince Naseem and Johnny Nelson. He also does an enormous amount of work with the area's under-privileged kids, for which he received an MBE. Brendan listened to what Paul was saying and then said: *"You can't just do nothing... you need a purpose!"*

And the more I thought about it, the more I realised how true this was. The acquisition of money, wealth or 'stuff', which is unrelated to activity or effort, is rarely, if ever, satisfying. Lottery winners become unhappy, not because they now have money, but because they have lost their previous purpose... achieving financial security and working to buy 'goodies'... and have failed to replace it with a new one. And maybe large sections of the wider population are similarly afflicted, albeit less acutely.

Just a generation or two ago, they were too tied up with their primary purpose of feeding, clothing and sheltering their family, to need other 'purposes' in their life. Today, in this country at least, that purpose has been broadly taken care of. And many people now see acquisition per se, as a purpose, and expect it to bring them happiness and fulfilment. They acquire some 'stuff', but it doesn't make them happy. But rather than conclude that 'more stuff' doesn't make you happy, they conclude that they're not happy because they simply don't have enough 'stuff' yet! But no amount of 'stuff' will ever be enough.

Now I know what Brendan meant by purpose. He spends a lot of his life helping young kids who might otherwise go 'the wrong way', find their own purpose in life. So his purpose is helping others find a purpose. But I have a broader definition, which encompasses what most of us should be looking for...

To Create, Make Or Do Something Better.

The 'something' you create or make or do better, could be a business, a job, a house, a product, a book, a charity, a club, a society, a plan, a person's life... whatever. Note that I said: 'create or make better' not 'buy'. Buying doesn't work. Money offers a convenient measure of how well your creation has done but, in isolation, offers little in the way of satisfaction or happiness.

So am I saying that making money is pointless? Not at all, but it has to be used in the right way if it's to have any impact on your level of happiness. I'll say it again: buying 'stuff' won't do it.

Money, once earned, opens up 'purpose opportunities' that aren't available to people without it. That might involve buying time to pursue a personal project, buying instruction to further your goals in a project or hobby, or directly investing in people or projects where money can be used to create something... or make something better.

This is the real way you can use money to create personal happiness... not through the vacuous purchase of yet more gadgets and gizmos that clutter up your life and render no long-term benefit. You 're-invest' the money in a purpose that has meaning to you and that will bring long-term satisfaction and happiness.

Now don't get me wrong, I'm not suggesting you have to give the money away, work for charity or help the disadvantaged. That might not be your thing. It might not be a purpose that is going to make you happy. Your purpose could be a totally selfish one... to work towards a personal challenge like climbing a mountain or sailing around the world for example... but there has to be something – a plan followed by action to create something – or make or do something better.

It's all about seeing something you care about transferred from an idea, to a plan, to action, through to an end result with a positive outcome. It's about having an impact on something.

What that thing is will be very personal to you... it may or may not require large sums of money to bring about. Only you will know. But the more money you have, the wider the choice of 'purposes' you will have.

The happiness-creating potential of money is not in what it can buy, but rather in the access to new purposes that it can bring.

You can't use money to buy happiness directly, but you can use it as an 'entry ticket' to the next level, and the best tickets – the expensive ones – offer limitless choice.

Look, I'm not totally stupid, I know that if you're struggling to make ends meet, you probably think the preceding 500 or so words is pure baloney.

"Just give me the cash," you may say, *"and I'll show you whether it will make me happy. Purpose my arse!"*

Nothing I can say will convince you that having a million or two to spend as you please won't make you happier than you are right now, or that if you were in that position, you couldn't happily sit on a beach for the rest of your days and conspicuously consume. Nothing will convince you of that other than experience.

As the great Spike Milligan once said: *"All I ask is the chance to prove that money can't make me happy."* That's why so much of this book is devoted to the task of helping you become financially strong and secure. The things I'll do to prove a point!

It's The Journey That Matters.

A key theme in just about every self-help or self-improvement book is goal setting, and it's easy to understand why. If you don't know where you want to go, how can you expect to find your way, or indeed, know when you've arrived? But it's a more complex process than you might think, and an over-emphasis on the achievement of goals is something of a red herring that can lead you along the wrong psychological track.

Your life is made up of a series of journeys. Sometimes you embark on them one after the other, and at other times they're concurrent. Each journey usually has a goal or target attached. It could be the attainment of a qualification, a promotion, a new job, buying a house or other asset, perfecting a skill or ability, building a saleable business, achieving recognition in your field, progressing a relationship to the next level, achieving financial security, or something else. It's perfectly natural to become focused on the destination but a big mistake to neglect the journey.

The nature of worthwhile goals is that they are rarely achieved quickly. The journey to each is what life is all about, but many people miss out on much of what it has to offer – because their focus is on where they want to go. The irony is that reaching the destination is almost inevitably an anti-climax. There is invariably an: *"Is that it?"* moment when you realise you've reached your goal and it doesn't feel how you expected it to. Few achievements can match the expectation and anticipation, and this feeling of slight deflation is then replaced with a realisation that this isn't the end of the journey at all; it's a brief stop-off before embarking on the next leg. Once you've arrived at one destination, it's vital that you immediately embark on another journey. There's no ultimate destination – not in this life at least. The journey is the thing.

All of this may sound negative, but it isn't. It's merely to alert you to the fact that the journey is what really matters. Destinations are merely brief stops on a longer route and it's only by going on the journey and experiencing the highs, lows, successes and failures along the way, that you can really appreciate the destination. So take the time to enjoy and appreciate the journeys you embark upon. By all means, garner all your efforts to reach your destination quickly and smoothly, but not at the expense of looking out of the window every now and again and stopping off to enjoy all the fascinating stuff along the route. When you look back on any achievement or goal you have reached it will be the journey you'll remember, not the ultimate destination. If you start out with the right attitude, it's within your power to make those memories great ones.

Overnight Success Is An Illusion.

You've no idea how lucky you are that I'm here today writing this, because if it weren't for Steve Ashman and the insatiable appetite of the Skegness slot machines, my life would almost certainly have taken a completely different path. I think I'd better explain.

Back in the days of flared trousers and platform shoes I harboured ambitions of becoming a pop star. I had the electric guitar, knew five chords (two more than Status Quo) and had practised signing my autograph to the point of inducing repetitive strain injury. I was ready. All I needed now was a band.

As luck would have it, I was surrounded by four equally deluded mates, one of whom couldn't play anything at all but who lived in a pub with a perfect rehearsal room. Obviously, he'd be the lead singer. We were ready to go – all apart from one thing.

Steve Ashman was to be our drummer – a drummer who had just one thing standing between him and rock super-stardom – he didn't own a set of drums. Rumour had it, that he'd once owned a set, but had traded them in at the local swap shop for some fishing tackle and an air pistol. Not a problem though. He'd saved £50 from his summer job on a burger van and would use that to obtain the missing piece in our jigsaw… just as soon as he returned from his holiday in Skegness. I think you can probably guess the rest.

When Steve returned from Skegness he didn't have a penny to his name, all £50 had been donated to the amusement arcade owner's benevolent fund. And that was it – the dream was over. The world had lost what would almost certainly have become one of the all-time great bands. And all for the want of a set of drums.

I was thinking about that while watching a TV programme called *Before They Were Famous*.

I'm sure you have probably seen it, or shows like it. The idea is that they dig into the archives and find footage of famous people before they made it '*big*', and here's what's interesting. No matter who the '*star*' is – no matter how they might seem to have burst onto the scene from nowhere, there's always plenty of footage.

One show featured, amongst others, Ricky Gervais, who nobody had either seen or heard of before *The 11 O'Clock Show* and *The Office*. And yet, there he was on a TV show from the early 1980s as a singer in a New Romantics-style group… twenty years before he became an 'overnight success'. It's the same story with all the *X Factor* and *Britain's Got Talent*-type show contestants. The impression given is that they've all just walked in off the street for their one and only shot at fame and fortune. But, once the winners have been chosen, the old video clips start to surface. And what you see time and again is evidence of a life dedicated to the pursuit of fame: childhood TV advertisements, small appearances in plays and soap operas, singing and dancing spots on various TV shows. In fact, anything which furthers their craving for fame.

The point I'm trying to make is this. It takes years of effort and sacrifice to become an overnight success. When you see someone burst from nowhere to great success, you're only seeing the very tip of a massive iceberg. And what lurks below the surface is the hard work and persistence that put that person in a position to break through and give the impression that it was all fairly effortless.

If by some miracle, I do become a star of either stage or screen, there would be no appearances on *Before They Were Famous* for me, because I've never done anything anybody ever thought was remotely worth filming! Contrary to my opening remarks, if I'd had even the slightest talent or aptitude for life as a rock god, I wouldn't have let Steve

Ashman's deficiency in the drum department hold me back. I'd have found another drummer, or raised the £50 we needed some other way. I'd have persisted.

Fact is, it was one of those daft pipe dreams that all teenage lads have, and I had neither the talent nor the commitment to even give myself a ghost of a chance of success. I gave up at the very first hurdle – it just wasn't easy enough for me. Overnight success is a perception for the audience, but never a reality for the performer.

I'm sure you're ahead of me here, but this holds true for whatever it is that you're striving for. There will be setbacks, failures and disappointments along the road to achieving success in every field. There will be an apprenticeship to serve, almost certainly some pain and anguish to endure.

But when you get there, when you reach your goal, all your 'audience' will see is the success. They won't see anything of what went in to achieving it.

A lot of people give up on what they're trying to achieve because they spend too much time in the 'audience'. Whatever field you're in, you nearly always spend quite a bit of time in the 'audience' before taking the plunge as a 'performer'. And from the audience's perspective, success is easily obtained. Just the tip of the iceberg is visible remember. Now, step over the threshold from audience member to performer, from spectator to player, from wage slave to businessperson and it all comes as a bit of a shock. The success doesn't come anywhere near as quickly as it appears to everyone else. You're still coming to this from the perspective of a spectator remember… a place where only the end result is visible. And so the temptation, the instinct, is to give up because your spectator's expectations have come up against the harsh reality of life as a player. And you're just not prepared for it.

I remember very well being totally demoralised when my first attempts at making some money by my own efforts (rather than just turning up and being given a salary at the end of the month) didn't get the results I felt they deserved. I looked around at the other people who'd stepped out of the audience to become performers, and couldn't believe that they were prospering so well while I was struggling. But what I couldn't see was the 'iceberg of struggle' that had already taken place for them in the past, and which to a certain extent, was still taking place on a daily basis.

I said earlier, that if I were to become famous, there would be no old video clips to show. Well I didn't become famous, but I have had some business success. There are no video clips, but there's plenty of evidence of earlier efforts to create an independent income that resulted in less than glittering success. There was the dating agency, and the CV writing business and the multi-level marketing business and the... no... it's too painful to go on!

Now to be fair, some of these efforts couldn't be called a failure... but just like Robbie Williams' appearance as a dancer on children's TV, they do look fairly pathetic in the light of what was to come later. But they were a necessary stage in the transition from audience member to competent performer.

Sadly, most people are so traumatised by the reality of taking the first steps to becoming a performer – it's so much more difficult than they expect – that they give up very quickly; often believing that the established performers must have had some lucky break or advantage they don't know about. How else can you explain the ease of their 'overnight' success?'

The answer is that all massive overnight success is the end result of years of 'invisible' experimentation, persistence and hard work. And there's little point in stepping out of the audience and onto the stage unless you're mentally prepared for that reality.

The Grass Is Rarely Greener.

My daughter's school choir wasn't behaving well, and their teacher wasn't happy…

"You lot are a disgrace," he complained. *"You only behave properly when there are visitors here. I went to another school last week and you should have seen those children. Well-behaved, polite and a pleasure to be around… not like you rabble. Why can't you be like that?"*

There was silence in the room, until one young girl, aged seven, had the courage to raise her hand. *"Yes?"* said the teacher, more than a little irritated. *"But sir,"* she protested, *"you **were** the visitor!"*

The seven-year-old had identified what millions of adults fail to grasp, that the grass only *seems* greener on the other side of the fence. When you get to look at it properly, more often than not it's just a brown and weed-ridden, as you perceive your field to be.

Most people are keen to create a positive impression. That means they tend to emphasise the positive and hide or suppress the negative when presenting themselves and their lives to others. As an outsider, you rarely get a realistic impression. You're not going to get a true picture of their school and you're not going to get a true picture of their life either.

It's very tempting to look at someone else's life, business, job or relationship with envy. From the outside it can look more fulfilling, simple, lucrative or whatever it is that you feel yours isn't. But you must always bear in mind that as a 'visitor', you can't possibly see the full picture. That can only come when you get inside, and stay there for some time – when you get beneath the beautifully presented veneer surface.

People who neglect what's underneath this veneer often spend their lives being seduced by the surface only to be disappointed by the harsh reality beneath. And what's worse is, they repeat the same cycle over and over.

The key is to understand that, in most situations, you're the 'visitor', and to treat what you hear, see and experience accordingly. This doesn't mean replacing open-mindedness with cynicism, but it does mean abandoning the rose-tinted specs. Equally important is the necessity to fairly evaluate and appreciate what you already have. It's a shame if you have to go to the trouble of clambering over the fence, before you can appreciate how green your own grass really is. And sometimes, the climb back over, is less than straightforward.

What You're Looking For
May Be Closer Than You Think.

If you've ever visited Edinburgh, I'd be prepared to bet you've also visited its castle. Most visitors do. It's one of the most photographed buildings in the UK and famous around the world. It's on the tick list of every self-respecting North American, Australian or Japanese tourist. So would it surprise you to learn that 20% of people living in Edinburgh have never visited it?

If I look out of the window right in front of me as I write, I can see *The Magna Science and Adventure Centre*. Whilst it's not quite on a par with Edinburgh Castle, it is one of the most popular tourist destinations in the North of England. And yet less than half the people in my office have ever visited it. They could walk there, and yet more have visited *Alton Towers* than the attraction on their doorstep. So what's going on here?

Between 1900 and 1925 a gentleman by the name of Russell Conwell delivered the same iconic speech around 5,000 times. And the fact that 20% of Edinburgh's residents haven't visited the castle, 50% of my staff haven't visited *Magna* (and someone sitting six feet from me right now has been to most corners of Europe, America and the Far East, but has never visited the Yorkshire Dales) suggests the message Conwell delivered, in that oft-repeated speech, is as relevant today as when it was first delivered. What's more, it's a message that could be the key that unlocks a number of financial, psychological and social treasure chests for you.

Conwell's speech centred on the apparently true story of a North African farmer who became frustrated at being poor. He heard tales of how other farmers had made millions by going out and discovering diamond mines, and got very excited by them. In fact he became so excited that he couldn't wait to sell his farm and go out prospecting himself. With his farm hastily sold, he set off to roam the African continent, searching for those elusive diamonds. He had no success, and several years later, tired, beaten and disillusioned, he threw himself in a river and drowned.

Meanwhile, things were going a little better for the man who bought the farm. One day, he was walking across his newly acquired land when he spotted an attractive blue and red rock on the bed of a small stream. He didn't know what it was, but liked the look of it and so picked it up, took it home and placed it on his mantelpiece as an ornament. A few weeks later, a visitor to the farm picked up the rock and almost fainted. He asked the owner if he knew what it was… he didn't. The visitor told him that it was a huge rough diamond – as it turned out the largest ever discovered – a fact that was of intense interest to the owner as there were hundreds of similar stones in the stream. The farm, which the original owner abandoned in search of diamonds, turned out to be the source of one of the largest diamond mines in the whole of Africa.

I'm sure you can see what pulls all this together. The human psyche default position seems to tend towards attempting to fulfil wants, needs and aspirations externally. The unwritten, underlying subtext is clear – the answers to our needs and problems are to be found far away. They can't possibly be close or we would already be benefiting from them. I can't pretend to understand the psychology of this, something to do with taking for granted what we already have and over-valuing what others have perhaps, but whatever it is, it creates it's own reality.

So what's to be done about it? Well let's stick with the farm analogy for a moment. Your farm might be a business, a job, a relationship, a house or something else that's important to you. Heck, it might even *be* a farm!

Have you really had a good look around your farm recently? Do you know everything that's there? Might there be undiscovered diamonds lying hidden in areas you haven't recently explored? Might the diamonds be in the rough and difficult, at first, to spot? Do you know anyone who might be able to help identify and then polish these rough diamonds? Do other farms only look good from a distance? Might the diamonds in other farms be just as difficult to harvest once you get there?

The truth is that when you see other folk showing off their diamonds, they don't necessarily have a better farm than you. But what they've learned to do is:

1. Search their farm properly
2. Recognise what rough diamonds look like
3. Polish these rough diamonds effectively.

You see, it's only when you've done all this that it makes sense to move off the farm. Every one of us is sitting on our own personal 'field of diamonds'. No two are exactly the same. Your knowledge, skills, experience, contacts, strengths, weaknesses, interests and preferences all determine your field's boundaries. And the great thing is that to mine this field, you don't have to go anywhere. Because the excavation tool you need is located right between your ears.

What You REALLY Want
May Not Be What You Think.

Hollywood legend Morgan Freeman didn't always want to be an actor. As a young black man growing up in the American South in the 1950's, you can imagine that he wasn't starting out with the best of advantages. But that didn't deter him, because what he wanted more than anything, was to become a fighter pilot.

He joined the US Air Force at age 16, as an engineer, and studied and worked hard until finally, at age 21, he was given the opportunity he'd dreamed of for so long – to train as a pilot. Given the prejudice and barriers in place at that time, this was an incredible achievement. But as he sat in the cockpit of the plane for the first time, a transformation came over him. A fundamental change took place. This wasn't what he wanted at all.

Freeman realised that he was sitting in a machine designed specifically to kill and destroy. That would be his job – his role in life. And that wasn't the idea he's fallen in love with. What Freeman had fallen in love with was some Hollywoodesque notion of what a fighter pilot was and represented – how they were seen, perceived and treated. He wanted to play the role of a fighter pilot, but without having to do what a fighter pilot does. He walked out on the US Air Force that day and never went back.

Here's another story. I suspect this one isn't true, but it further illustrates the point I'm hoping to make.

A boat docked in a tiny Mexican village. An American tourist complimented the Mexican fisherman on the quality of his catch. *"How long did it take you to get those?"* he asked. *"Not so long,"* said the

Mexican. *"Then why didn't you stay out longer and catch more?"* asked the American.

The Mexican explained that his small catch was quite enough to meet his needs and feed his family.

"So what do you do with the rest of your time?" asked the American. *"I sleep late, fish a little, play with my children, and take a siesta with my wife. In the evening, I go into the village to see my friends, have a few drinks, play the guitar and sing a few songs. I have a full life."*

The American interrupted. *"I have an MBA from Harvard and I can help you! You should start by fishing longer every day. You can then sell the extra fish you catch. With the extra revenue, you can buy a bigger boat."*

"And after that?" asked the Mexican. *"With the extra money the bigger boat will bring, you can buy a second boat and then a third boat, and then more until you have an entire fleet of trawlers. Instead of selling your fish to a middleman, you can then negotiate directly with the processing plants. Pretty soon you could open your own plant. You could leave this little village and move to Mexico City, Los Angeles, or even New York! From there you could direct your whole enterprise."*

"How long would that take?" asked the Mexican. *"Twenty, perhaps twenty-five years,"* replied the American. *"And after that?"* mused the fisherman.

"Afterwards? Well, my friend," laughed the American, *"that's when it gets really interesting. When your business gets really big, you can start selling stocks and make millions!"*

"Millions? Really? And after that?" said the Mexican. *"After that you'll be able to retire, live in a beautiful place near the coast, sleep late, play*

with your children, catch a few fish, take siestas with your wife and spend your evenings drinking and enjoying your friends."

We all have goals and aspirations. We often spend years dreaming about them and working towards them, but without giving a great deal of thought to the key questions…

Why do I WANT this? Do I REALLY want this?

These are uncomfortable questions because they get right to the heart of who we are, what really motivates us, and what we really want out of life.

Morgan Freeman discovered that he didn't actually want to be a fighter pilot, he'd just bought into a myth about what a pilot was and wanted the status, prestige and standing that a pilot enjoyed. The Mexican fisherman realised what the American tourist couldn't yet see… that he already had what great wealth would bring – the time and freedom to live exactly as he pleased. He didn't need to invest the 20 years of blood, sweat and tears to become wealthy to get the benefits he wanted. So what about you?

What are you dreaming about or working towards? If it's a particular business or career, do you really want to go into that business or career? Or when you think deeply about it, are you doing it to garner some social or financial benefits that you feel will come with it. And if that's the case, is there some (perhaps easier or more palatable) way you can enjoy these same benefits without spending a huge portion of your irreplaceable life working towards something you don't really want?

Morgan Freeman discovered his outlet through acting. The Mexican fisherman was smart enough to realise that he already had what he wanted. Very few people do this – unless they happen to be fictional characters, created to make an important point! So again, what about you?

What do you really want? Is it to be at the top of the ladder you're currently climbing? And even if it is, might there be another ladder somewhere else that gets you exactly where you want to be without the steep climb or the feeling of vertigo when you get to the top. These are questions that only you can answer, but I hope I've at least given you a reason to ask them.

A Fair Day's Work For A Fair Day's Pay Is A Loser's Game.

A friend of mine's son was doing his A levels and looking for a part-time job. The only thing on offer was a position 'flipping burgers' (his Dad's description, not mine) for just over minimum wage at McDonalds. His dad advised him not to do it because the wages were too low. It was slave labour, he said. And so he didn't take the job. So was he right or wrong?

In the real world, effort and reward don't always correlate, as you would hope. Sometimes you get paid poorly for doing a lot of work and, at other times, you get paid very well for not doing very much at all. And the killer fact is that the former, more often than not, precedes the latter.

People with what I'll call 'an employee mentality', simply don't appreciate that maximising long-term success is rarely achieved by maximising short-term revenue, or matching it exactly with short-term effort. Another way of looking at this is that you often have to give before you receive – and that there may be a significant time delay between giving and receiving. What's more, you won't receive proportionally from everyone you've given to.

My friend's son could have gone to work for McDonalds, hated every minute, took his meagre wages and slumped off home again. Alternatively, he could have recognised that he was working for the most successful business of its type in the world and that it must be doing something right. If he learned what that was, then maybe… just maybe… he could use that knowledge to boost the profits of his own business one day, or enhance his performance in a better job with another company.

Maybe he'd have learned nothing of value at McDonalds and left within a month to join another company… and then another… and then another.

He might have gone through nine companies that paid him poorly and taught him nothing, before arriving at the tenth that still paid him poorly, but provided the key to a golden future. Can you see why sulking over the lowly wages wasn't really a sensible option to take?

There are a myriad of ideas and beliefs which mislead and hold people back, and one of the most insidious is the insistence on doing a fair day's work for a fair day's pay. Very few people who have achieved real success in life have ever done that. Effort and reward have rarely been in sync for them. But I make this statement with the important proviso that they have nearly always done a lot of work for which they were not paid or were under-rewarded, before receiving those big rewards. It rarely, if ever, works the other way around.

If you're committed to maximising your success in the long term you should shun any thoughts of a 'fair day's pay' and move to a more holistic approach, where total effort over an extended period is measured against total reward. Now that doesn't mean you should be a mug and let people and companies take long-term advantage of you. But it does mean that you should look at everything you do in terms of the long-term potential benefit, rather than purely in terms of the short-term cash-in-your-pocket-today reward.

What You've Heard About Eggs And Baskets Is True.

This is absolutely central, to your financial well-being in the years to come. It will shape and determine what happens to you. Do I have your attention? Good. Let me ask you an important question. Who has control over your financial destiny – you, or someone else?

Let's get one thing clear – no matter whether you're employed, unemployed or self-employed the only person you want to control your financial destiny is you. Why? Because nobody else cares about it like you do. In fact, probably nobody else cares about it at all! Do you want your financial destiny in the hands of someone who doesn't much care about it, and won't suffer unduly if it all goes pear-shaped? I know I don't!

But what do you do about it? After all, you can't control an employer, a major customer, a competitor, the government, a legislator, or any one of the dozens of people and organisations who can lay waste to your carefully laid plans. What you can do, however, is make sure your house of cards doesn't come tumbling down. And that means it's absolutely vital that you spread your financial eggs around a number of baskets – baskets that are subject to separate external influences out of your control, which can screw you up. So start developing separate income and profit 'baskets' or centres. Far better to have five sources of income, each bringing in £10,000 a year, than one big one yielding £50,000. As the saying goes: *"Don't put all your eggs in one basket."*

If you have several profit centres, each with a different set of controlling external factors, your position is far safer. If one job, business or profit centre is hit, the others are unlikely to be, because their fortunes are governed by different factors.

If you do nothing else in the next 24 hours, sit down and assess how secure your financial position is, and who's controlling it. If you have just one source of income or profit, the chances are it isn't you. That's not a comfortable position to be in and will almost certainly come to bite you sooner than later.

You're As Strong As Your Weakest Link.

On the night of April 14th 1912, during her maiden voyage, *RMS Titanic* struck an iceberg and sank two hours and forty minutes later in the early hours of April 15th. At the time of her launch in 1911, she was the largest passenger ship in the world and regarded as the safest. The sinking resulted in the deaths of 1,517 people, making it one of the worst peacetime disasters in maritime history and by far the most famous. But what caused the unsinkable to sink?

It's been the subject of much controversy for decades. Some have blamed a faulty rudder, while others have cited navigational errors. But according to new research, the key factor in the ship's sinking may have been the use of sub-standard rivets.

The 'rivet theory' was first raised in the 1990's, no pun intended, but was denied by Harland and Wolff, the company that built the ship. Now, historians have uncovered evidence that the company was forced to compromise on quality as it struggled to build three huge ships at the same time. Faced with a regular supplier unable to cope, they turned to smaller forges producing less reliable products, to make up the shortfall.

RMS Titanic was deemed unsinkable because it was designed to stay afloat, even if four of its watertight compartments were flooded. But when it hit the iceberg, so many rivets popped along the starboard side that five compartments took on water, and the ship went down. And so it seems that this most famous of ships succumbed to the truth of a well-worn saying: *"A chain is as strong as its weakest link."* No amount of engineering or technology could overcome a deficiency in a small, but critically important part of the ship.

What's true of *RMS Titanic* is true of you. Are you confident that the 'rivets' in your life are strong enough to withstand some unexpected impact? Or have you perhaps cut corners along the way, gambling that you can avoid any nasty icebergs? The bottom line is that you can't afford to neglect any area of your life (and health is particularly critical) in pursuit of what you see as more important goals. Any shortcomings will eventually find you out and sink all your plans.

There's No Such Thing As A Negative Event.

I'm sure you've heard the old saying: *"It's an ill wind that blows nobody any good."* Like me though, you've probably not given it a great deal of thought, or considered what you can learn from it.

Ill winds don't come much worse than tornados. Despite being an incredibly destructive force, there is a positive side if you look hard enough. For example, there was a gentleman called Tetsuya Fujita, of the University of Chicago, who has made a career out of 'twisters'. He is a world expert, and the scale on which the severity of a tornado is measured carries his name. Thanks to tornadoes, Fujita's place in history is assured. Without them nobody would know who he was, and he may never have made his mark. Tornadoes have benefited others too. Numerous film-makers, TV documentary teams, authors and photographers have enhanced both their professional reputations and bank balances as a result of work associated with these killer winds.

When news of a tornado is reported in the press or on TV, everyone focuses on the cost. It's always portrayed as a negative event, which is understandable. But one man's cost is another man's revenue. The cost of clearing up after a tornado doesn't disappear into the ether. It goes into the pockets of the enterprising individuals and companies who make it their business to deal with such matters. The following news story illustrates this…

"Great news today from Jackson County, Texas, where a tornado ripping through several large towns has created a boom for construction firms in the area. A spokesman for the local trade association estimated that $30 million of work would be coming the way of local building firms, and at least 1,000 short-term jobs will be created. Local hospitals also

reported record business, with billings to insurance companies likely to approach a five-year high."

I'm sure you realise that I'm using tornadoes as a euphemism for just about any *"negative"* event. The point is this – for any negative side to an event there is always the other, more positive, side... a positive side for someone. The task is to identify that positive side and capitalise on it.

Let's look at more examples. War and international conflict are universally regarded as negative. Yet for many – those involved in the production of armaments for example – war is good and peace is bad. It's the other side of the coin that we rarely look for.

Understandably, when my office was broken into, I wasn't in the mood to appreciate the positive side of the ever-increasing crime figures in this country. However, the companies I subsequently paid to install an alarm system and roller shutter doors were probably better placed to do so.

Then there's the economic recession, which is almost universally viewed as negative. Yet in any recession there are winners and losers. Reduced property, equipment and stock prices will provide an economic springboard to many new ventures.

Redundancy is also perceived to be a negative event. And yet an equally valid interpretation is to see it as an opportunity to make a fresh start, allowing time to find a new, more fulfilling path, and there may be a hefty redundancy payment to finance the search. Many people go through redundancy and find a far better paid, more fulfilling job than that which they lost. *And* with their redundancy payment still intact.

There isn't a single *'negative'* event that doesn't have a positive side – yes, even death, as any undertaker or florist will testify. The important thing is to identify the positive aspect to events and put yourself on the right side of the fence.

You're Just Like Everyone Else... Well Almost!

If you want to understand the needs, wants and motives of others – and it's critical to optimising your life outcomes that you do – there's a really easy way to do it. When you realise what it is, you'll be amazed you didn't figure it out before, but you'll also, more than likely, be a little disillusioned.

You see, people have been telling you that you are unique since you were a small child, and on the surface, you are. Scratch below that surface though, and we all share pretty much the same wants, needs, hopes, desires and motivations. So when you're trying to figure out what that other strange person you're dealing with really wants, it isn't difficult. Their underlying wants are the same as yours, although they may be manifested in slightly different ways.

We'll be looking at what some of these wants, needs and desires later in the book, but for now hold on to the idea that the people you're dealing with each day are just like you. When you're trying to figure out 'where they're coming from', a little introspection will usually deliver the answer.

You're Fully Responsible For What Happens To You.

To succeed in any effort, it's essential that you accept full responsibility for the outcome. Starting out with any other attitude almost guarantees failure. Teenagers who are told that their criminal behaviour is a result of social deprivation will carry on, secure in the knowledge that it's someone else's fault. Employees who think they have a poor boss will hold back, knowing they can blame him when it goes wrong. Business people who believe that the economy is dying on its feet will stop investing, secure in the knowledge that their failure can be laid at the Government's door. It is all depressingly self-fulfilling.

Don't deceive yourself. Whatever ventures and endeavours you undertake – accept responsibility. *The outcome is down to you… no excuses.*

As soon as you do this, a miraculous thing will happen – your chances of success will multiply. It's easy to blame someone else, but not so easy to blame yourself. When there's someone else to blame, it's so tempting to give up at the first hurdle. *"The bank wouldn't give me any money,"* you may say. *"The customers didn't see what a good product I had,"* or maybe, *"My colleagues let me down,"* and *"There's just too much competition out there."*

When you accept full responsibility for the outcome, you won't give up: *"Let's try another bank… and another,"* you now say. *"Let's see how else we can sell it,"* or *"I'll make up for my colleagues shortcomings."* Also maybe: *"How can we provide a better service than the competition?"*

Colonel Sanders, at the age of 66, approached over 2,000 restaurants with his idea for Kentucky Fried Chicken before he found one that would give it a chance. How many would you have approached? Five? Ten? Most of us would have given up long before, not blaming ourselves of course, but rather the damn fool restaurant owners who wouldn't know a good idea if it jumped up and bit them. Sanders took full responsibility. He had no intention of blaming anyone else, and as a result, he had no reason to.

Twelve publishers turned down J K Rowling before she found one that would publish her *Harry Potter* books. It would have been so easy for her to bemoan the fact that the publishers just wouldn't give a chance to a single mum writing adventure stories, primarily for boys, and give up. She didn't, she took responsibility. And now she's at least £400 million richer!

Do yourself the biggest favour you can. Take full responsibility for the outcome of every project you undertake from day one. Your successes will be all the sweeter and your failures all the more rare.

You Can Do It – Probably!

Henry Ford once said: *"Whether you think you can, or you think you can't – you're right."* There's a great deal of truth in that, but it has to be tempered a little if you're to avoid chasing pipe dreams.

If someone of similar background and abilities has already done what you hope to achieve, then, of course, you know you can do it. That's why finding appropriate mentors and role models *is* important – more about that elsewhere. But, if it hasn't been done already, the jury is out and you have to make an appraisal of whether what you want to do is realistic. It would be wrong to talk down your prospects here – you are capable of far more than you can imagine – but as anyone who has ever watched a TV talent show will testify, there are far too many people chasing 'goals' which will never come to fruition.

In truth, there are very few areas where talent puts in place an immovable barrier – entertainment, sports and music spring readily to mind – but unfortunately these are the areas where unrealistic aspirations tend to flourish. The good news though, is that very few career or business paths require innate talent or skills that a determined and motivated person can't learn. Though, as Henry Ford recognised, even the most realistic goals will wither in the face of a lack of belief.

It's Okay To Be Different!

The words 'eccentric' and 'millionaire' seem to be almost inextricably linked in the popular psyche. I'm not sure where it all started – maybe it was with the reclusive Howard Hughes, or the money-conscious John Paul Getty I – but the tag has stuck. Anyone with a few quid in the bank and a liking for stripy trousers automatically inherits the label. And the implication is often less than flattering – that the person may be rich, but they're not quite normal. Well of course they aren't!

Here's how Webster's Dictionary defines the word eccentric:

"Deviating from an established or usual pattern or style."

Of course millionaires deviate from an established or usual pattern or style! This is an essential pre-requisite to achieving anything worthwhile – not just making a lot of money. Why? Because to bring about extraordinary results requires extraordinary actions. What do you think happens if you conform to an established or usual pattern or style? That's right – you get a normal or usual result. And a normal, more ordinary, result doesn't lead to great achievement. If it did, we'd all be great achievers.

Do you have a tendency to conform and follow the crowd? If you do, you're far from alone (there wouldn't be a crowd otherwise!) and in all likelihood, it's a hangover from your childhood.

Before we're out of nappies, we're already being indoctrinated to believe that there is a 'right way' to do everything. We are led to believe that among the many 'wrong' ways of doing something there is just one right way. Of course, when you're a kid it makes a lot of sense. The world is a new and complicated place. The last thing you need is 12 different options for holding a spoon! And so we learn one way, and that's the right way.

When we start school, the same process continues. One way to write, one way to read, one way to add up, one way to sit, one way to queue for lunch, one way to hold hands with your partner on the odd outing from school. One way for everything and one way for everyone. And so it goes on. Every schoolbook we ever read told us the right way to do things. Rarely were we given a choice or options. *"This is how it's done and this is how we'll all do it,"* they seem to say.

Is it any wonder then, that by the time we approach adulthood this whole idea has become firmly embedded? There's a right way to do things, and it's the only acceptable way. To succeed, you have to do things that particular way. Take any other path and you'll fail. The ultimate conclusion, of course, is that there's one way to think.

This 'one right way,' middle-of-the-road approach keeps most people safe. They are safe from harm, reasonably competent in what they do, and importantly for the rest of us, comfortable to be around. We know what they're going to do and when they're going to do it. There are no surprises, nasty or otherwise.

However, as an approach geared to maximising individual potential it's extremely flawed. While conventional wisdom, the 'right' approach is usually safe, it isn't necessarily correct. Follow it and the result will inevitably be mediocre. Why? Because everyone else will be doing the same thing. Follow them and you'll get the same result. Mediocre, middle of the road and very average.

Most successful people not only behave differently to the norm, they also think laterally, outside the box. And that is what separates them from the herd. So remember – whatever path you choose there is no one 'right' way – there are a number of ways that work. Your task is to find the one that suits you best, not the one someone else says you should take. To borrow a popular phrase, dare to be different.

There's A Place For You.

The inhabitants of the Japanese Okinawa Islands, on average, routinely expect to live – and be healthy – well into their nineties. The reasons aren't totally clear, but it's thought to be something to do with the traditional soya protein-based diet, and the fact that the people there tend to eat very little by Western standards.

The fact that the people thrive on that diet and lifestyle is down to heredity – what their ancestors have experienced and endured throughout the centuries. Their bodies have geared up, and adapted, to thrive on it. But, if you or I were to take up the same regime, we wouldn't necessarily get the same results. This is borne out by what happens when the young inhabitants leave the islands and adopt the more urban lifestyle of the city. When they move to a more Western-based lifestyle, not only do they lose all the benefits of their heredity, but they also fare worse than their contemporaries, who have been brought up in that urban environment. Their life expectancy actually falls below the average. They have evolved to thrive in a completely different environment. Their heredity offers no benefits in the new environs of the city, yet massive ones on their native Okinawa Islands.

There's a lesson here that stretches way beyond the health and longevity arena. We all have skills, attributes and predispositions, and if we're not getting the results and outcomes we want, it could be because we're applying them in the wrong environment.

A Formula One car is awe-inspiring on a track, but wouldn't get you out of your own street in the real world. A 50cc scooter would be totally useless on a motorway, but would get you around the centre of London better than most vehicles. Average natural abilities, applied in the right environment are far better, and more effective, than outstanding abilities applied in the wrong one.

So you need to work towards finding the environment or arena that is best suited to your predispositions. No matter how clever, talented or able you are applying your innate and acquired strengths in the wrong environment renders you the proverbial fish out of water – or the Okinawan living on fast food.

If ever you've felt yourself under-achieving, the reason could lay here.

You're Intelligent You Idiot.

On a clear night, if you look up at the constellation of Orion, you may notice at its base a bright blue-white star called Rigel. With a luminosity of about 40,000 times greater than our sun, Rigel is the sixth-brightest star in the sky. Its surface, at 11,000 Kelvin, is surrounded by a gaseous cloud, which was either shed by the star's own pulsations or arrived as a result of stellar wind.

Rigel isn't the furthest star from Earth, but, at around 765 light years away, it's not what you'd call 'on the doorstep' either. Light travels at 186,282 miles per second, so every second since King John signed the Magna Carta in 1215 light has been travelling, from Rigel to Earth, through space at that incredible speed. And the light your eyes will detect on that chosen clear night will have only just got here.

I don't know about you, but I find this sort of thing fascinating and mind-boggling… literally mind-boggling. Like a lot of people I suspect, I attempted to read Stephen Hawking's *A Brief History Of Time* (which is supposed to simplify all this stuff) and got about as far as page 26. My brain just doesn't seem to work in that way, and I'm constantly amazed and impressed by those people who can work out all this detailed information about something further away than I can imagine. It's beyond my comprehension. And yet many of these same people would struggle to put up a shelf, find their way to the next town, run a hot dog van, or the hundred and one other things which other folk find easy.

You see, we all have things we're good at and things we do badly. It's very easy to become intimidated by what we perceive to be great intelligence. The truth though, is that most of us have great 'intelligence' – just not necessarily the sort that we traditionally associate with the word. Einstein has a lot to answer for.

Mention the word genius, and his is the name that comes to most people's minds first. Because of this, mathematics and science seem to have hijacked intelligence, with the result that the rest of us end up feeling... well a little bit thick. The knock-on effect is that we somehow feel that, the sort of intelligence that can unlock the secrets of the universe, is what really matters.

The reality though, is that other types of intelligence are just as important – maybe more so if your goal is to make a success of the comparatively mundane matter of life on Earth. As impressive as the ability to calculate the mass of a distant star is, it's not really going to help you build a career, a business, a relationship or anything else with your feet planted firmly on Earth.

If you haven't already done so, I'd urge you to firmly nail down exactly where your peak intelligence and predispositions lay – and then stop worrying about what you can't do, and focus all your efforts on what you do best. When you combine a strong predisposition with something you enjoy, you have a massive head start on the competition. You might not be able to explain the stars – but that doesn't mean you can't reach for them.

You Must Make Every Scene A 'Take'.

A few years ago, I was executive producer on a film, and spent a few days on the set. On one of those days I got roped in as a supporting actor, an 'extra', and I spent much of the day doing the same thing over and over again. Needless to say, I didn't have much of an idea what I was supposed to be doing. I couldn't work out whether we were rehearsing or filming, so I asked Colin Salmon, the actor who was in the scene with me. His reply contained an important message with far wider implications.

"I don't know," he said, *"I never concern myself with it… I just do it every time as if it's a take. You never know what they're going to use."*

Can you say you live your life like that – giving it 100% in every scene? Or do you sometimes allow your game to slip when you think it's not important, when nobody's looking, or when you think the audience isn't worthy of your very best effort? What's true on a film set, is true in life. You never really know when the important cameras are rolling – when you're in a potentially life-enhancing situation, or in the company of people who have more to offer you than you could ever imagine. It's only with the benefit of hindsight, when you see the film being played back, that you realise you missed a massive opportunity by assuming it didn't matter, when it clearly did.

The only solution is to do what Colin Salmon does – start out with the assumption that every situation, every meeting, every interaction is a 'take', the one that's going to be used and may have a lasting impact on your future. That has implications for the way you dress, the way you look and the way you conduct yourself. Give it 100% every time. When you do, there are massive benefits not just for you, but for everyone you come into contact with.

First Impressions Will Make Or Break You.

So there I was sitting at my desk, when one of the office staff came in looking very worried indeed.

"There are two blokes asking for you in reception," she told me, *"They wouldn't give their names… said you'd know who they were and what it was about."*

"Hmmm, I'm not expecting anyone," I said, *"What do they look like?"* *"BIG…"* she exclaimed, with slightly more emphasis than I was comfortable with, *"…and MEAN!"*

"Could you go back and ask them if they'd be good enough to give you a name," I said, trying desperately not to appear too unsettled. She went away, and came back a minute later with two names dutifully scribbled on the back of an envelope.

"It's okay," I said, more than a little relieved, *"they're harmless… at least to me."*

I've known Dave, the gentleman who thought it would be fun to terrorise my office staff and me, for about 20 years or so. He's been involved in a variety of jobs and businesses, but has never quite fully moved away from the field he was in when I first knew him. Let's call it 'security'.

Anyway, Dave moved on in the 'security world', and ended up working for what I can only describe as a sort of '*SAS*' of nightclub doormen. If a new nightclub was opening somewhere, or a club was experiencing a lot of trouble, Dave and his team were called in. He explained it to me like this: *"We set a standard on the door."*

I knew exactly what he meant. The last thing a club needs is trouble, or a reputation for trouble. Because there's nothing that breeds trouble like... trouble! It's a bit like when you were at school. When a new teacher started, there were always a few kids who would push the boundaries... just to see how 'easy' this new teacher was going to be. If they couldn't cope, then word quickly got around and pretty soon, everyone would be giving them a hard time. But if they responded quickly and firmly (and especially if they could throw in a little fear for good measure) they'd be able to nip trouble firmly in the bud before it even started. Once again, word would get around, and their classes would be a haven of calm.

I had a maths teacher called Mr Jenkinson. The first lesson we ever had with him, he scared the living daylights out of us all. He seemed to be in a perpetual state of fury, ready to explode at the slightest provocation. He did that for one lesson only. After that he was fine. Nice bloke, good teacher, no problem. And there was absolutely no hassle in his class.

It was about three years before we realised that first lesson had been an act. Nothing more than a strategy to create an expectation... an expectation that was to endure long, long after the apparent reality of unexploded fury. And Dave and his colleagues were sent in to do exactly the same thing.

When a new club opened, the owners knew that there would be local youths determined to test the boundaries, and in some existing clubs, those boundaries had been tested and found to be weak. What Dave and Co. set out to do was create a clear indication of where the boundaries were, and what the outcome would be if they were ignored or broken. In short, they were there to create an image and expectation, that the doormen at that club were not to be messed with, and that the consequences of doing so would be severe.

This process would take maybe a couple of weeks, and then they'd move on to the next new club or trouble spot requiring the shaping, or reshaping, of customer expectations. But the really interesting thing is what happened next.

Because you might expect, that once the 'SAS' had gone away, their deterrent effect would diminish or disappear. But that rarely happened. Once the image and expectation was in place, it took on a life and reality of its own, irrespective of the personnel who were doing the job.

It works like that with school kids, it works like that with drunken youths, and it pretty much works like that with all the rest of us too... the image and expectation will endure long after the reality has been confined to history.

First impressions are vitally important. They are enduring, and take on a reality of their own. Once an image or an expectation enters someone's psyche, it takes a lot of shifting. So it's vitally important that the first impression you create in every given situation is precisely what you want it to be. Note that I don't say a 'good impression', because that might not necessarily be what you want. Dave and Mr Jenkinson (my maths teacher) were aiming for fear and respect. It may be in your interests to create impressions of intelligence, likeability, competence, sophistication, caring, 'ordinariness'... or something else. But whatever the desired impression is, you have to be right 'on the ball' with it from the very first few seconds of meeting the person or people you're hoping to influence.

Start off on the wrong foot and you'll have an almost unwinnable battle shaking off that erroneous first impression and creating the one you want. But get it right from 'the off', and your path towards whatever you're hoping to achieve will be so much smoother.

90% Of Success Is Turning Up And Persisting.

I once watched a superb wildlife programme about the African honey badger. As the name suggests, this animal is particularly fond of honey, and with the African bush being notably short of branches of Sainsbury's, the only source of food available to the honey badger is beehives – with lots of bees in them.

Watching the honey badger go about its work was fascinating. Having located a hive in a hollowed out tree it cleared out debris to make a wider entrance. The reason would soon become clear – it was going to need an escape route, and it knew it.

The first foray into the hive was painful to watch. It was attacked systematically by the bees and got only a small mouthful of honey before withdrawing to lick its wounds. At this point you expected the honey badger to give up having learned a painful lesson. Not a bit of it! Time after time it went back into the hive, getting stung each time and only getting small amounts of honey in return. You almost found yourself screaming: *"For God's sake, don't go back in!"* as another visit resulted in more pain.

But as time went on, a funny thing happened. The stings got less and less as the stinging bees died off, and the honey badger came away with more and more booty on each visit. Eventually, the bees gave up the fight and the honey badger made off into the bush with the entire hive worth of honey. Victory, from what initially appeared to be a hopeless quest.

The honey badger knew the job wasn't going to be easy from the start. He knew he wasn't going to get something for nothing, and that pain would inevitably precede pleasure. But what he also knew was that if he kept at the job, if he persisted, eventually the resistance would be broken down and his goal would be reached. Of course, he had an alternative. After going into the hive for the first time and getting stung so badly for so little he could have thought: *"This isn't worth it. I'll go and find an easier hive."* But he didn't, because he knew that all hives are difficult, and if you want the honey you just have to buckle down and do what's necessary.

I'm sure the lesson of this isn't lost on you. Many people give up when entering 'the hive' for the first time, after receiving the inevitable 'stings' and getting very little in return. They decide to go and look for another 'hive' where the bees aren't so fierce. When that 'hive' proves equally difficult, they give up again and go to the next, and the next, and the next. Entering every 'hive' involves getting stung, and so they get hurt again and again, and with very little reward because each time they're starting on a new 'hive' where the defences are at their most intense.

For 'hive' read goal, target, endeavour or venture. For '*sting*' read problems, difficulties, or obstacles, and you'll get the picture. No matter what you hope to achieve, there will be difficulties, and they will be at their most intense in the early stages. Giving up to look for something easier when these difficulties present themselves will prove to be a fruitless exercise. The next venture will carry with it a whole new set of difficulties for you to deal with.

A few years ago I worked with a salesman. He had an almost God-given knack of alienating, upsetting and offending everyone he met. He had any number of ways of achieving this. You would almost think it was deliberate, but I don't think it was. This man's sales figures were actually the best in the company, by quite some margin – not what you'd expect from someone who was guaranteed to disenchant every new prospect within seconds of meeting them.

Intrigued by the paradox, I was pleased to have the opportunity to accompany the man on some of his sales calls. At first I thought that he must deal with his customers differently to everyone else. Not so! He was equally obnoxious. So how did he succeed? Simple really. He asked everyone whether they wanted to buy, even when it was patently obvious to anyone with an ounce of sensitivity that they did not.

When they told him they weren't interested, he ignored them. When they told him politely to leave them alone, he pretended not to notice – or maybe he didn't notice. Then he asked them again, and kept asking until they said yes. I'm convinced that some people ordered just to get rid of him, but order they did. When it comes down to it, all that he had in his favour was a skin like a rhinoceros, and the tenacity to ask as many people as possible whether they would like to buy his product.

The bottom line is this. Unless you're very lucky, success will not happen straight away. It takes time. Not one successful person has ever had a 'clear run'. You're unlikely to be the first. James Dyson, inventor of the Dyson vacuum cleaner, and now owner of a business worth several hundred million pounds put it this way: *"Success is made of 99 per cent failure. You galvanise yourself and you keep going."* Persistence is what saw him through in the end – just like the honey badger – and it will do the same for you.

You Don't Need To Do The Thing Right – Just Do The Right Thing!

Many years ago when I had a proper job, I had a colleague whose work rate left me astonished. Whenever I saw him he was scribbling away at some paperwork or other. If I phoned him in the evening he would lose no time in telling me how I had interrupted his battle with yet more paperwork. Occasionally, we would meet up at conferences and sales meetings. It was the same story; paperwork scattered across his hotel room, and him cursing his luck that he didn't have time to enjoy the hotel facilities.

I found all this a bit disturbing. You see, I was supposed to be doing the same job as him, and all this paperwork was something of a mystery to me. Mine took about 20 minutes once a week. *"I must be doing something wrong,"* I thought, but I couldn't work out what it was. All the same, my friend didn't seem to be making any great strides in the job, despite holding it for some 15 years. In fact, his results were worse than mine.

A few years later I was working for another company, where once a year we would get together to prepare annual budgets. It was not an exact science to say the least. The unknown factors were such that the final figures could never be anything better than a wild approximation. The whole process was supposed to take three days. By midday on the first day I had my budget complete, only to watch with increasing levels of dismay as my colleagues took another two days to complete the same job. This was worrying. They were able people, and as someone with considerably less experience, the most sensible conclusion was that I must be at fault in some way. But the end result seemed okay, and my budget proved to be at least as accurate as that of anyone else.

It took me quite some time before I figured out the important principle that underlies these apparent anomalies, which is this: It is far more important to 'do the right thing' than it is to 'do the thing right'.

Most people are more concerned with being seen to be doing the thing right, rather than stopping to consider whether they're doing the right thing in the first place. In other words, the first decision should be to decide upon priorities and the value of tasks before undertaking them. There is little or no point in carrying out a job to perfection that doesn't need doing, or one which isn't particularly important in the overall picture. Far better to carry out that job to an appropriate standard and devote maximum time and effort to the things that really matter.

Taking time to establish whether you're doing the right thing, before doing the thing right, will make an enormous difference to your life in the long run.

You Must Question Everything!

A friend who's a retired senior fire officer told me an interesting story…

One day, he was out on routine fire inspection duties with his team. They walked into a branch of one of the major high street banks, asked to see the manager, and announced the purpose of their visit. The manager appeared from his office and eyed them up and down suspiciously.

"How do I know you're who you say you are?" he said.

As you might imagine, my friend considered this to be a somewhat strange question to ask of five men dressed in full fire-fighting gear, but he understood the need for caution and decided to humour the manager. He led him to the window and pointed outside, where a shiny red fire engine was parked at the roadside. *"There,"* he said. *"£75,000 worth of state-of-the-art fire-fighting equipment."*

"Hmm," murmured the manager. *"Have you got a card or something with your picture on it?"*

We all do things on autopilot – without thinking. It's how we get through the day and one of the easiest ways to do that is to follow standard procedures, rules and regulations. What would you consider to be the most convincing form of ID? A laminated card, which any self-respecting crook might have forged, or five tons of fire engine? It seems obvious, doesn't it? And yet the bank manager's 'autopilot' procedure was to insist on an ID card.

He probably didn't consciously think about the reason why he should ask for an ID card. As you know, banks need to establish identity as quickly and as certainly as possible before divulging account details.

Instead, he just made the cerebral leap from visitor to ID, without asking himself the question... '*Why?*'

Now I know you might laugh and think that you wouldn't be so inflexible or unthinking and maybe you wouldn't. But at the same time I'm sure that there are rules, regulations, procedures and ways of doing things in your life that you are currently following – rules which are no longer appropriate due to changed circumstances.

Whatever you're doing, I guarantee you'll be following procedures laid down by others before you. You will be doing things using the methods established by your predecessors. And I'd wager that you've probably given little or no thought to – or even have no knowledge of – the thought processes that went into creating these procedures in the first place.

So question all the rules, procedures and methods that you're presently using in the important areas of your life, and ask yourself...

- Who created them?

- What was the thinking behind them?

- Are they still relevant today?

- Has anything happened over time to make this rule or procedure obsolete?

- What do you think would happen if you broke the rule, changed the procedure, or didn't carry out the procedure at all?

- Are you doing things this way because they've always been done like this – or do you have a better reason?

When you start to examine and question everything you do, and why you do it, I think you'll be amazed by what you'll find.

What You Can't Do Doesn't Matter.

Many people give up on an idea, a dream or a goal, because they view some disadvantage or disability or inability as an insurmountable barrier. It could be a physical barrier like an injury, a practical barrier like the absence of a particular skill, a social barrier like chronic shyness, or a cerebral barrier like the one imposed by dyslexia. Whatever the barrier, the result is the same – acceptance and capitulation.

But here's something that's interesting – think of the most competent and able person you know, and the number of things that person can't do will greatly outnumber the things they can do. Can they speak Swahili, or fly a helicopter or carry out open-heart surgery? You get the idea. There are thousands of things that even the most able individual is incapable of doing.

What's important is how they focus upon, and capitalise on, the things they can do. And that seems to be the key – finding what you can do well, and then focusing on and specialising in that. That doesn't mean ignoring a disadvantage or disability. Rather it means recognising it for what it is – just one more thing to be dealt with in the best way possible. How do you do this? By focusing on what you can do and getting help with everything else.

So many great scientific, literary, medical and social advances would never have come about if their creators had focused on their weaknesses. So many great entertainers and sportsmen would never have triumphed if they'd yielded to a 'disability'. So many of the great fortunes in history would never have been made, if those involved hadn't recognised the fact that even the most able, rarely have all the skills needed to reach a goal without help.

It would be a great shame if you gave up on a goal or ambition because of a disadvantage that might easily be overcome and compensated for.

Failure Is Good. Fail Small; Fail Quick; Fail Often!

I want to tell you the tale of Billy Blunderbuss and Tommy Treadright. Both were aspiring parachute designers and both thought they had a winning idea for a new, improved parachute.

Now I know what you're probably thinking – these are not real people and are in fact fictitious characters with silly names chosen for their comedic value. Perish the very thought. Billy and Tommy are as real as they need to be and have a great deal to teach us.

Billy is (or should I say was) true to his name and a bit of a blunderbuss. When he had an idea, he wanted to get on with things. He was a man to 'go for it'. So when he came up with his parachute idea, he drew it out on a scrap of paper and then spent every waking moment for over a year, making a full-sized prototype. It looked great and he was confident, so he hired a small plane, instructed the pilot to fly to 5,000 feet and jumped out with the parachute strapped to his back.

Who knows what went through his mind as he pulled the ripcord and it came off in his hand, but it couldn't have been good. Billy plummeted to the ground and made such a hole that they couldn't decide whether to dig him out, or just fill it in and put a stone on top. By any measure, things hadn't gone well.

Now Tommy took a different approach. He drew his parachute on paper and then entered the characteristics into an aerodynamics program on his computer. The program quickly flagged up that the parachute wouldn't work in its present form, so Tommy redesigned it. The program now suggested that the parachute could work in principle and so Tommy created a small, scale model of it. He attached the parachute to a weight and threw it off a stepladder. The model worked reasonably well but the descent was far too fast. In real life, anyone using it would probably break his or her legs. Tommy made some adjustments, and over a period of weeks, honed his design so that eventually the descent was about right.

Heartened by this, Tommy hired the same aircraft Billy had used. The pilot, still traumatised from hearing Billy's screams as he plunged to the ground, was relieved to learn that Tommy had no intention of jumping out of the plane yet. He'd made a life-sized dummy that he intended to hurl out at 5,000 feet. They both watched as the parachute opened but then got blown out of shape as the wind got hold of it and caused it to malfunction. The model crashed to Earth at around 30mph and was smashed to pieces.

Undeterred, Tommy went back to the drawing board, and made another prototype, and then another and then another, as each was put to the same test and found wanting. But he didn't give up, and eventually, he arrived at a design that seemed to work perfectly. It was ready for a full live human test... a test that Tommy didn't carry out himself. After all, if there WAS a problem, he needed to be around to put it right. As his 'test jumper' floated serenely to the ground, Tommy breathed a sigh of relief. It had been a long road, but he'd got there in the end. Success!

But this story isn't about success: it's actually about failure. So let me ask you this... who's the biggest failure in this story, Billy Blunderbuss or Tommy Treadright? And what does that tell us about the nature of failure? Before you answer I want to make a confession.

I may have given you the impression that I'm a success, but if success and failure are at the opposite ends of the spectrum, I'm not sure that description is either fair or accurate. You see, although I have many of the things that people associate with success, I have to admit that I've also had (and continue to have) more than my fair share of failures. If someone looking at you and I from the outside were to judge me to be more successful than you, I'd be prepared to bet that I fail more often than you do. And if that same person were to judge you more successful than me, then there's every chance that you have more failures than I do. Isn't that strange and counter-intuitive? The more successful you are, the more failure you're likely to experience.

So going back to our friends Billy and Tommy, who's the biggest failure? Well, in terms of sheer volume of failures it has to be Tommy. His computer model failed, and his scale model failed several times, as did his full-sized model. Billy only failed the once. But Tommy ultimately succeeded and Billy didn't. Billy's failure was a big one.

Over the years, much of the correspondence I've received from people desperate for success has focused on failure... experiences of it, fear of it and their desperation to avoid it. And when these people talk of failure, they are usually referring to the sort experienced by Billy Blunderbuss... total, complete and final. But what Tommy Treadright teaches us is that there's another kind of failure, which isn't nearly so negative. It is a failure that is planned, controlled, limited in scope and, if properly managed, can ultimately lead you towards success rather than away from it.

Almost all significant success is preceded by small failures. So the goal isn't to avoid failures, but rather to manage the scale and nature of them so that they move you closer to where you want to be; so they aren't so catastrophic that the big prize is lost altogether. I think misunderstanding this causes more dreams and endeavours to wither and die than anything else, because if you're dead set on avoiding failure at all costs, the safest thing to do is... nothing! And when you do nothing, you don't fail, but you don't succeed either.

Something you may not know about me is that I have a totally unblemished record in the boxing ring. I have never been beaten. I have never failed once. But the absence of any Lonsdale belts or a bank account stuffed with prize money – the spoils of success – tell the other side of the story. I have never tried. And not failing is not the same thing as succeeding.

At least Billy Blunderbuss didn't fall in to the trap of doing nothing, but his approach was still fatally (literally!) flawed. He set himself up to fail big, and that's what most people do. And to make matters worse, they usually set themselves up to fail slowly as well. Failing big is bad. Failing slowly is bad. Failing big and slow is the worst combination of all. Sadly, this is something that happens all the time…

People put plans in motion for a massive all-or-nothing assault on a goal or target. Because the effort is going to be massive, it's going to take a lot of money and time to get to the point of 'take-off'. The success or failure of the entire venture rests on this one all-or-nothing event. If it fails, it's a catastrophic failure of Blunderbuss proportions. All the money is gone. The time is gone. There's no way back.

The solution is to structure your approach so that when you fail, (and you almost certainly will at some point) you fail small and you fail quickly. Small and quick failures become minor correction points on the road to success rather than the Armageddon scenario that is characteristic of their large and slow counterparts. Anyone can fail big and slow, but it takes careful planning, and an acute awareness of the steps you need to take to reach a goal, to fail quickly and fail small.

The idea of aiming to fail fast and small will probably not mean the same in your life as it does in mine, but it's worth investing some time and effort figuring out exactly what it does mean. While Tommy Treadright is enjoying the spoils of his success, Billy Blunderbuss is languishing six foot under without anyone having to call on the services of a doctor or a gravedigger. They both tried, they both failed. But I know which one I'd rather be.

Standing Still Is Impossible.

It's a massive mistake to assume that the things that work for you today will always work. You need to constantly monitor all the important areas of your life and make changes where necessary. When times are good it's very easy to become complacent. Perhaps you've worked hard to get where you are in your career, your business or personal life and you just want to enjoy what you have. You want things to stay just as they are. I'm sorry, but they won't.

Change is absolutely unavoidable and inevitable. It's impossible to stand still! Marking time simply isn't an option. Without any doubt whatsoever, if you stand still, stay the same, and do the things you've always done, you'll go backwards... and you'll keep going backwards until you disappear into oblivion. The only way to stand still, or maintain your current level of success, is to move forward. And the only way to progress is to move forward even faster.

Change is going to happen so it's vital that you keep an eye firmly on the horizon so that you can see change coming well in advance, and take the appropriate action. Once you're in the 'thick' of change – once it's forced upon you – taking optimal action is much harder to do.

There's No Need To Feel Guilty If You're Winning.

If you achieve success, financial rewards will follow. Others will try to make you feel guilty or uncomfortable about that. They'll question whether it's right for you to have so much, while others have so little. You'll need to settle this firmly in your own mind if you're to reach your full potential. No rational person with a conscience will go all out to get something that they believe is morally wrong.

Employment has seldom been less secure. Even previously 'safe' jobs in the Civil Service and Banking are disappearing at an alarming rate. State benefits are being eroded away too. It's very unlikely that anyone currently under the age of 40 will receive a state pension, for example. You need to make independent provision for your own financial well-being.

The concept of a 'caring and sharing' society is a very attractive one. But it has never existed and sadly, it never will. It's a convenient media invention that flies in the face of basic human nature. If you fall on hard times, the only person you can rely on is you – with some help from your immediate family… if you're lucky. Regrettably, no one else will either care or share.

The wealthy have always realised this. Whatever the prevailing media-inspired 'mood of the nation', they have continued to do what they have always done… accumulate as much money as possible, in the shortest period of time – and hang on to it. Immoral? Well the wealthy are without doubt the biggest contributors to charities and other good causes. They are the greatest generators of wealth, through the creation of employment that didn't previously exist. Individual wealth is never created without simultaneously creating wealth for others. And the rich are also (with the exception of a few 'bad apples') the largest contributors to the coffers of the Exchequer, which is precisely where the state benefits come from to look after the people who either can't or won't make provision for themselves. Think about it!

You need to feel no guilt in aiming for success and the financial rewards that come with it. By doing so, you are helping yourself, your family and the country… and yes, even the people who either choose to rely upon, or are forced to rely upon, others to provide for their welfare.

The Rich Aren't Evil
And The Poor Aren't Saints.

Wealth and moneymaking has a real public image problem – and it's not hard to see why. Newspapers are littered with stories of 'fat cat' bosses, and greedy bankers ripping off the public. Film, TV and literature almost always portray the rich guy as 'bad' and the poor guy as 'good'. Think about it for a moment. The rich guy is almost always the nasty villain of the piece, and the poor guy is the one we all end up cheering on.

You might never have thought about this. You might not think it matters. But it does. Because this completely fabricated image develops a reality of its own when it enters the psyche. Large swathes of the population really do believe that the rich are 'bad' and the poor are 'good'. They may not think it consciously, but the impression is there. And if you think that the wealthy and successful are somehow 'less nice' than the poor, why would you want to join them? Why would you work through the inevitable trials and tribulations that will precede the transition?

The truth of course, is that there are 'orrible people right across the wealth spectrum, from rich to poor. A rich person is no more likely to be unpleasant than a poor person. Many wealthy people do good things, as do many poor people. For every rich person ripping off his employees and his customers, there's a poor person (and maybe more than one) robbing your house or attacking you in the street.

There's absolutely no virtue in poverty and no evil in wealth. Bear that in mind at all times as you go through life, because you'll encounter many who either consciously or subconsciously, will try to persuade you otherwise.

You Have To Get Rich Sometime, So Get It Over With.

A recent survey encouraged respondents to ask the one question they'd like answered above all others. The most common question was: *"How do I make a million pounds?"* I was thinking about that when I saw the results of some other research that suggests that people's 'happiness quotient' doesn't rise once their income goes above about £25,000 a year in the UK.

So there's a bit of an anomaly there. People want to know how to get rich, but they're unlikely to experience any enhanced happiness, should they achieve that goal. So what's going on?

The answer, of course, is that a good many people believe that they'll lead a more happy and fulfilled life with a million or two in the bank – no matter what any research suggests. Are they right? Well I recently heard an interesting quote, which might give a clue to the truth. It comes from a controversial mystic called Osho. Anyway, here's the quote:

"Everyone should own a Rolls Royce. You can see God better from the seat of a Rolls Royce."

Let me explain what I think he meant. In 1954, Abraham Maslow published his ground-breaking work on personality and motivation, which introduced the concept of the hierarchy of needs. I won't go into the detail of that here (far too boring!) but the basic idea is this:

Humans have a hierarchy of needs which motivates them – starting from the physiological needs (hunger, thirst, shelter) and then moving on to safety and security needs, and then social needs before arriving at the need for self-actualisation. That's the need to do the thing or things you really want to do – what you feel you were born to do.

I've simplified this an awful lot, but the important point is this... each need has to be satisfied in order before moving on to the next. So safety and security only become important when you've solved the hunger, thirst and shelter issue. The need for love and self-esteem only kick in as a motivator once you're comfortable you're not going to be murdered in your bed. And so on. So what's this got to do with anything?

Well, I believe that slotted into the modern-day hierarchy of needs (somewhere between safety and self-actualisation) is the desire to own big houses, fancy cars and lots of toys... to be rich! And even though this stage is pretty universally accepted to be futile in the quest for happiness (for those who have passed through it at least) it's such a strong desire in most people in the Western world, that it totally obscures the view of what lies beyond.

So going back to the quote from Osho, let me paraphrase it in words that make more sense to me:

"Everyone should be wealthy, because you can see what's really important when you're wealthy."

Once the desire (need?) to have enough money to buy all the stuff you could ever dream of has been satisfied... and you realise that it's not all it's cracked up to be... you can start the search for that 'something else'... the next need. Almost everyone with more than a dozen brain cells does this. What that something else is, will differ from person to person, but it will almost certainly be tied up with a need for self-esteem, achievement, and in the words of Maslow – self-actualisation. Most of us can't identify it though – and it doesn't therefore motivate us – until the 'get rich' need (whatever that means to you) has been fulfilled.

There's Very Little Correlation Between Education and Earnings.

If financial success is important to you, pay close attention. In my naive formative years I thought I'd got it cracked. It was simple. Everyone told me how crucial education was. Get a good education, go to university, get good qualifications and the money will follow. After all, if you're better qualified (brighter?) than 95 per cent of the population, you'll make more money than 95 per cent of the population right? Well not quite.

I'd got a couple of things wrong. Many of the positions that a first-class education prepares you for are not particularly well paid. Become a teacher, a local government executive, a librarian or a civil servant and you won't starve, but you might not make much more than a long-distance lorry driver with nothing more prestigious than a HGV licence to his name.

Even what seemed to be 'really well-paid' jobs didn't (and still don't) offer much potential for the accumulation of wealth. A GP earns around £75,000 a year, an average head teacher around £60,000 and a provincial solicitor around £50,000. All of these are well above the average, but offer no chance of millionaire status. Just work it out. If any of these people were to save all of their salary (what would they live on?) and pay no tax at all (that would be nice!) how long would they have to work to accumulate a million pounds? It's not going to happen is it?

I well remember coming out of college to the somewhat disconcerting sight of one of my former classmates (he was actually a long-standing member of the remedial class, but it was the same school) pulling up in a brand-new Jaguar. All bought and paid for legitimately with the profits from the three successful businesses he'd set up while I was still reading about it!

Many of the financial heavyweights of the past two decades owed little of their success to education. Richard Branson left school at 16 with a few low-grade O levels. Alan Sugar, George Walker and many like them graduated from what is often called: 'The University of Life'. What was true in the past twenty years will be true in the next. Some of the biggest financial successes will come from people with few qualifications.

A Good Education Can Hold You Back.

The last thing I want to do is to encourage you to neglect formal education, but there's no doubt that it's not right for everyone, and in certain cases can actually hold you back. Education often constrains people, forcing them down paths that their qualifications dictate they should take – the 'professional' path – rather than the one they would otherwise choose. Heavy pressure is frequently placed on well-qualified people to not 'waste' their education: *"You've qualified for it, so you're going to do it!"*

Although Charles Dunstone, co-founder of The Carphone Warehouse attended an expensive public school, he never shone academically, and took a job in sales rather than go on to university. *"If you leave school with few qualifications,"* he says, *"you've got nothing to lose, and you're quite happy to go and set up a business. If you're more successful, you go and join Arthur Andersen (Management Consultants that are now part of Deloitte Touche) or something. Me, I was working as a salesman. If this hadn't worked out, I could have got a very similar job and lost absolutely nothing."* Education gives you something that is very dangerous – something to lose. It can stop you doing what you really want to do in favour of what you feel you should do.

So am I saying that education is totally counter-productive? Not at all. The information gathering and analytical skills acquired in higher education, combined with real-world skills, resilience and pragmatism, can create an almost unstoppable force. But education on its own won't do it for you, and might actually prevent you going down your 'right route', if you're not alert to the dangers.

Faking It Can Help You To Make It.

Back in the bad old days when I had a 'proper job', I worked as a glorified salesman for a training publications company. Although the company had a reasonably sized US parent when I joined, the UK operation consisted of two salesmen, two secretaries and the managing director, Barrie Johnson.

Anyway, from time to time, he would accompany me on customer visits, and it was a great learning experience for me. You see, one of Barrie's firmly held views about himself – one of the things he was always most definite about – was that he couldn't sell. And yet you only had to spend five minutes with him in front of a customer to see that nothing could be further from the truth. A combination of olde world public school charm, and some of the most effortless 'spin' I've ever witnessed, had the customers almost literally eating out of his hand.

It was all so easy for him. He would wax lyrical about the company; his creative team, his editorial team, his research team, his print department and his 50,000 square foot warehouse and office complex, and they would lap it up. But none of it existed… or at least it didn't exist in the way he was presenting it.

The 'creative team' was a local graphic designer, the print department was a jobbing self-employed printer from South London, and although the warehouse did exist, about 50 other companies shared it. (I think we had four bays.) Barrie didn't tell lies, he just painted a carefully crafted picture, and just left enough room for people to fill in the gaps for themselves in a positive way.

Anyone visiting the company back then, would have found two

secretaries working from three small offices above an estate agent's branch; a very different picture from the one Barrie painted.

I once sat in a meeting with him at a large government agency, where he invited the Director to come down and meet up with his creative and research people. I was horrified, because I knew there was nobody to meet. When we got outside, I asked what he would have done if the Director had accepted his offer. *"They never do,"* was his reply. And of course, he was right.

I learned a valuable lesson in those meetings, and it was this – you are what people believe you are. And what they believe has less to do with the truth than what you present yourself to be.

Now, I suspect you may be mumbling words such as, 'honesty' and 'ethics' at this point, and I can understand that. But I'm not talking about doing something with the intention of ripping someone off, or doing him or her a disservice in any way. I'm talking about doing something that will enable you to show the world that you can deliver first-class value. How can you do that if they won't even give you a chance because they think you're too small, too unskilled or too inexperienced?

Just about every successful entrepreneur has a tale to tell about how they were creative with the truth with regard to their size, success or experience when they first started out.

Some have hired flashy offices by the day; others have borrowed expensive cars to create an impression. And then there are those who have persuaded friends and family to stand in as 'satisfied customers' or toadying underlings in the presence of a hot prospect. There are many ways of creating an impression of size, success or experience. And here's the really interesting thing…

This whole process is devastatingly self-fulfilling; because more often than not, you become what you purport to be. You present an image of size, success and experience; people give you a chance to prove yourself and you become bigger, more successful and more experienced – just as long as you deliver on your promises.

Look at it this way... you're doing the world a big favour. If you hadn't 'massaged' the reality a little bit, it would never have felt comfortable enough to give you a chance to do what you now do to make it a better place.

Fake it before you make it ethically, and you'll be given more opportunities to prove yourself in all aspects of your life. But do it unethically and it will get you precisely nowhere. You see, in the short run, you can mislead people as to who you are, but in the long run, you can't mislead them with respect to what you're able to do for them. And it's that which is the difference between long-term success and failure.

You Need To Adapt To The Real World.

There's an old picture postcard I remember first seeing as a child, that, for some reason, has always stuck in my head. There are two boxers standing in a ring. One has quite clearly been badly beaten. There's blood coming from his nose, he has two black eyes, and there are cartoon stars twinkling above his head. The other is completely unmarked. The beaten fighter turns to the victor threateningly and says: *"Just wait till I get you outside!"*

The joke is an obvious one. Here's a bloke who's lost a fight, threatening the guy who's just beaten him. Plainly ridiculous… or is it? A conversation with my friend Geoff Thompson, a martial arts expert, former nightclub bouncer and streetfighter, suggests that postcard wasn't such a joke after all.

Geoff explained that what works in the controlled confines of an organised sport will not necessarily work on the street. Martial arts and boxing skills do not translate to the street in their unmodified state. In his various books, Geoff tells many stories of how highly skilled and qualified fighters have been found wanting when coming under attack from an untrained opponent in real-life conditions – conditions where there are no rules, no limits – and where the attacker will almost certainly use tactics and techniques that are alien to the fighter. He says that many highly skilled, highly qualified fighters are walking around with a false sense of security. They have trained for attack scenarios that are not going to take place in the real world and are chronically unprepared.

What's true in the tawdry world of brawling is equally true in life. Many moons ago, I got a degree in business studies. That was my 'black belt', if you like. Just like someone with a black belt in karate, I thought it would be enough to out-fight and out-manoeuvre any 'inferior' competition that might come my way. You know, those poorly educated people who weren't smart enough to get a degree, people who had learned what they knew through mundane experience. Was I in for a shock!

You see, just like those trained fighters, I'd prepared for a battle that was never going to take place in the real world – or not in my world, at least. The techniques and strategies that looked so plausible in the classroom, simply didn't stand up to the demands of the real, practical world where things could get complicated – and the rules, boundaries and limits were just not where the theory I had learned told me they would be.

Many people make the same mistake. They believe that a qualification or a skill is going to be their passport to riches (or something they desire), when all it really is, is a ticket to stand on the starting line of a very long race. They cling to the belief that the hard work and effort they've invested in developing their skills and knowledge should automatically bring its own reward. They are better qualified, better trained and more skilled than most, and so wait for the moment when the rest of the world realises the fact and rewards them accordingly. It will be a long wait.

In the meantime they look disdainfully at the poorly qualified, the poorly trained and the relatively unskilled that are metaphorically beating the living daylights out of them every day. People who are able to do it because they know that the practical is better than the theoretical, that function is more important than form, and even half-arsed, ill-conceived action will beat meaningful contemplation most of the time.

The people who turn their skills or qualifications into 'real-world' success are those who recognise that all they have is an entry ticket, and then set about shaping and adapting what they can do and what they know, to the imperfect conditions that exist in the market. If you ever feel that your skills, qualifications and training haven't taken you where you deserve to be, perhaps the reason lies here. If you ever feel that your lack of skills, qualifications and training form an impenetrable barrier to success, then you now have cause to think again.

You're Not Underpaid.

Many people believe they're underpaid. They're not, and neither are you!

We're lucky to live and work in a free labour market. If you're not happy with the terms and conditions of your employment, it's within your power to do something about it. You can ask for more money, leave to move to a better-paid job or start your own moneymaking enterprise. Nobody is forcing you to stay in the job you're in at the current rate of pay.

However, if you can't negotiate a better deal with your employer, can't get a better job locally, aren't prepared to relocate to a better job elsewhere and don't have the wherewithal to start your own business, then the hard news is that you're not underpaid. You're being paid exactly what you're worth in the marketplace today.

Now you might not be paid as much as you'd like, or indeed as much as you can comfortably live on, but that doesn't mean you're underpaid. No employer, from either the private or public sector, is under any obligation to pay you more than you're worth in the market. And if you're still working for them at the current rate, that's precisely what you're worth. Believing that your level of pay is anyone else's responsibility but your own is self-defeating. If you want to be paid more, it's up to you to take action.

You Have To Believe
Or You'll Never Achieve.

It is extremely unlikely that you will achieve anything of note without first believing it can be done. The only exception is things you manage to pull off by accident. If you don't believe something can be done then it can't – not by you, at least. Why? Because your belief will affect your actions, which in turn will ensure you get the results you expect – good, bad or indifferent.

Read the biographies of successful people and you will find this as a recurring theme. Whatever they achieved they achieved twice – first in the mind and later in reality. Of course you will find the odd clown who stumbled across success, but they are the exception rather than the rule. Just to be very clear, without belief you will never take the actions necessary to succeed. So get into the habit of putting your belief system in place first.

Everyone Needs A Role Model.

Success seems to come in clusters. Liverpool, Bradford and Bristol are three UK cities with roughly comparable populations. How many footballers, comedians and pop stars can you name originating from each? Unless I've judged this badly, Bradford and Bristol are going to be tough, but Liverpool will keep you busy for hours. So what's going on here? Is it something in the gene pool, or is there something in the water in Liverpool that sets it apart?

If you dig a little deeper you'll find that the concentration of talent goes even further. Many of the successful footballers and entertainers attended the same schools and were brought up in the same districts, albeit many years apart. The key to their success becomes clear; it's belief. If someone else just like them has done it, they can do it too.

If you have some talent and you were born just around the corner from where a Premiership footballer was brought up, and who maybe even went to your school, why would you think anything other than: *"I can do it too"?* And if you think this, might you train just a little bit longer, practice just a little bit harder – in fact just do a little bit more of everything necessary to bring about success? Of course you would. That player becomes your role model: he bolsters and underpins your belief.

Now you know how this works, it becomes comparatively easy to 'fake it'. You might not know of anyone who achieved what you hope to achieve in your school, street or village, but you do know of people who came from very similar schools, streets and villages who have made it. Make it your business to learn as much about them as possible. Study their life stories. If they did it, so can you. You can take a free ride from 'The Liverpool Phenomenon', without even having to visit. I'll leave you to decide whether that's a good or bad thing!

Mentors Can Drive You Forward.

Whatever you want from life or wherever you wish to go, the chances are that someone has been there before and done it – or something very similar. A common theme that runs through the life stories of successful people is the use of mentors.

Arnold Schwarzenegger started out with few useful attributes for what he ultimately achieved – high-level success in four very different careers in the United States. Coming from a relatively poor family in a small Austrian town, and speaking no English wasn't a good starting point. His Ace card though was to recognise where his shortcomings lay, and to systematically eradicate them through the use of mentors.

When his goal was to be the world's best built body, he sought the advice of the very best bodybuilders. When his focus shifted to business, he studied and shadowed one of America's biggest magazine publishers. When he wanted to go into film, he made it his business to get to know the most successful producers, directors and actors. And when politics beckoned he headed straight for his in-laws, which is pretty useful when they're the Kennedy clan.

When you're clawing at the bottom of the tree, it's easy to take the view that those further up won't be interested in you and will rebuff any requests for information or advice. Some will of course, but many won't. Successful people often get a kick out of helping others to follow the path they've taken.

If you know what you want to do, find others who have already taken the same path and get in touch. With modern communications, it's easier than ever to do just this. Approach them in the right way – with courtesy and respect for their time – and the level of help and advice that you receive may well astonish you.

Chasing Money Is A Sure Road To Misery.

For most people, choosing a job, career path or business purely on the basis of the level of pay is unlikely to end happily. You will spend a great deal of your adult life at work, and the misery which results from being stuck in a role you hate will always override any financial advantages that ensue. No matter how much money you're paid, you quickly adapt to it, and it soon ceases to be a source of pleasure and satisfaction. However, it's a lot more difficult to adapt to spending huge chunks of your valuable and irreplaceable life doing things that give you neither pleasure nor satisfaction.

Find out what you really want to do and work towards that, irrespective of the perceived financial rewards – and don't worry about the money. If you have aptitude for your chosen path, it will find you! Your commitment and enthusiasm will ensure you rise far higher than you would have if you'd chosen a seemingly more lucrative, but less appealing, route. There are significant rewards to be had in most fields for those who rise to the top. Far better to climb to the top of a tree you love, than languish half way down another that you merely tolerate for money.

Your Parents Aren't Useless – Probably!

Every generation thinks that it's smarter and more capable than the one that went before, and yours is no exception. It seems to be part of the human condition. But your parents weren't always the boring, staid and world-weary folk you see before you. They were young once and they had hopes, dreams and aspirations, just like you. Now the harsh realities of life may have put paid to some of those, or they may have achieved everything they wanted, but either way, you have much to learn from them.

The truth is that your parents care more about what happens to you than anyone else on Earth. They want you to prosper. And they have not got to where they are without learning some valuable lessons – even if they are chiefly centred on what doesn't work! They yearn to be able to steer you away from the mistakes they made and towards the things they know will enhance your life, if you'll let them.

At the moment you probably feel they are old and out of touch, but give them a chance. Okay, they may be oblivious to Facebook and Twitter and seem unable to operate the latest technology without help, but their knowledge is based in more important stuff that you can't stick in a box adorned with an Apple logo. Technology changes but the fundamental principles behind successful relationships, social interaction, careers and businesses, do not.

Ask about your parent's life experiences and what they've learned, and two great things will happen. This will not only enhance your relationship immeasurably – everyone likes to feel valued, and your parents certainly do – but you will also almost certainly learn some things that will benefit you. You don't have to accept or act upon everything they say, their specific wishes and goals for you will probably not match your own, but just keep an open mind. Listen. There are few people who reach their early middle age and can't say: *"My mum/dad was right about... and I wouldn't listen."*

Well-meaning Friends Can Be Dangerous.

It's natural to discuss ideas, ambitions and plans with people you're close to. We all do it. But taking advice and guidance is something different. It's one thing to take advice from someone who has already followed the same or similar path. It's quite another to alter your plans on the basis of an 'off the cuff' comment from someone who has little or no knowledge, and whose opinion is based on nothing of any substance. They will often have heard of someone who tried 'something similar,' but it didn't work out. Not only that, but they ended up bankrupt, on benefits and eventually committed suicide while in a pit of failure-induced depression! So be warned.

Haven't you read about and researched what you have planned? Don't you know a great deal more about it than the person you're discussing it with? Then why on Earth would you put their opinions above your own? Politely listen, but be sure to separate out hard facts from hearsay, vagaries and plain twaddle. All this assumes of course, that the advice you get from those around you is well meaning, if inaccurate. It's not necessarily the case. Everyone has their own hidden agenda and it almost certainly won't be the same as yours.

Ben may well be your best mate, but it doesn't stop him being jealous of the fact that you've got a great idea. Perhaps he failed in something a few years ago and now it looks as though you're going to succeed. What better way to stop that happening than to pour cold water on your idea? Your partner may love you but it doesn't mean that they want to spend more time alone while you pursue your goal in your spare time, does it? What better way to stop that happening than to run down the idea?

Do you understand the point I'm making? Other people will have all sorts of reasons for discouraging you, which have little or nothing to do with the viability of your plans. To give up through this kind of discouragement is a crying shame and a waste.

Perception Creates Its Own Reality.

I don't know what life at your school was like, but at mine there was certainly a strict hierarchy to things. I'm not talking about the unimportant peripheral activities like performance in maths, English and science, but rather, the altogether more crucial matter of your ability to fight.

The 'rankings' were very clear to all with the best three or four enjoying a level of status and respect, which I wager they've never been able to match since. The 'cock of the school' was Stewart Rowe, a big fat lad, with a mean, ugly face – though I would have been reluctant to tell him that at the time. His position at the top of this particularly scabby tree went both unquestioned and unchallenged. And that's the interesting thing.

In five years, I never saw him have a single fight. Not once in all that time was he called upon to defend his position. Now that I think about it, none of the other 'top contenders' ever got into fights either. And yet their positions in the hierarchy never changed. So what have these musings about my school days got to do with reaching your goals?

Well, the key force at work here is that of perception, and it's such a powerful force, that it creates its own reality. Stewart Rowe had successfully created the perception in others that he was someone to be feared, which may, or may not have been true. That perception then took on a life of its own. Other people acted as if it were true, to the extent that nobody ever challenged the perception.

I'd even take that a stage further. If the perception had been challenged – if someone had taken a swing at him – the challenger would have been at a serious disadvantage, irrespective of any tangible factors that might affect the outcome. He would have been adversely affected by the perception. Subconsciously, the challenger would have expected to take a good beating.

This phenomenon was certainly evident in the early boxing career of Mike Tyson. Opponents were beaten before they had even got into the ring. But once the perception had been shattered by a brave opponent, subsequent challengers approached fights with Tyson in a much more positive manner, and fared far better as a result.

The bottom line is that you are what other people believe you are in all meaningful senses. If you create a strong enough perception, it's very unlikely that it will ever be challenged, and if it is, then the psychological advantage will very much belong to you. Creating and achieving success relies very much on creating a positive perception of the characteristics that are key to you achieving your goal. So decide what it is that you most want to be, create the compelling perception that it's true, and the reality that you seek will be all the more likely to follow.

'Successful Shammers' Can Mess You Up.

One piece of advice given to young people is to learn from, and emulate, successful people – those who have already made their mark. This is sound advice; in fact I've given the same advice to you elsewhere in this book. But there's a problem. How do you know who these people are?

On the face of it, it seems simple. Look at where they live, the car they drive, the lifestyle they appear to lead and you'll find the achievers who can help lead you down the path to success. If only it were that simple! I was reminded of this when on a recent trip to the United States, I came across a book entitled *The Millionaire Next Door* (Longstreet Press) by Tom Stanley and Bill Danko. It makes fascinating reading. The authors studied millionaires from 1973 onwards and found that they are far from the easily identifiable, conspicuous consumers most of us have been led to believe.

Most of the successful people in Stanley and Danko's study avoided showing off their wealth altogether. They were more likely to drive a second-hand Ford than a new Ferrari or Bentley. They shunned designer clothing in favour of 'off the peg' chain store items and expensive jewellery was not high on their list of priorities. Most lived in fairly modest houses and ate out at mid-range restaurants.

One thing they all had in common was that they lived well below their means. Only their bank accounts would give a clue to their true wealth, and nobody saw those.

If that's the situation in the United States, where the prevailing attitude to wealth and success is to admire it and aspire to it, how do you think the truly successful in the UK behave, where the attitude is much more negative? You don't have to think too hard to realise that what you see is not necessarily what you get. In fact, it sometimes seems that everyone is trying to create an impression completely at odds with the truth.

Most people who come to my office with some proposal or other arrive as the very picture of affluence and success – in an impressive car, a Mercedes, Porsche, BMW or the like, and wearing expensive designer clothes. Yet almost without exception, something very interesting emerges as our meeting progresses. They don't have any money! I don't mean they're not rich. I mean they're worse than flat broke. Their car is on finance, they're mortgaged up to the hilt and they can't even find a few hundred pounds to get their idea off the ground. And yet to the outside world they're wealthy and successful – people to be emulated.

On the other side of the coin, rarely a month goes by without a newspaper article being published about some apparently penniless old man leaving a fortune in his will. Nobody knew of his vast wealth or how he acquired it. It is these low-profile success stories that are the most fascinating and potentially revealing, not the half-truths put forward by the fast-car, fast-talking merchants.

By all means mix with, learn from and emulate successful people, but first make sure that they're the genuine article. To do so, you're probably going to have to dig below the surface. They could just as easily be driving a Renault as a Roller, just as likely to be living in a maisonette as a mansion. Face value holds no value.

The Best Thing In Life ISN'T Free!

You've probably heard the saying: *"The best things in life are free."* There's a strong element of truth in it, which makes it all the more damaging. Why? Because many people use sentiments like this as justification for sloth. If the most important things in life can't be bought, what's the point of working hard to build a career or a business? Well the very best thing in life isn't free at all.

A number of years ago, I met a well-known sports personality who had become a multi-millionaire as a result of his success. And yet this guy had virtually no interest in the things a great deal of money can buy. For him, most of the things that were really important cost nothing – the love of his family, the satisfaction gained from his work and the opportunity to enjoy the wonders of the natural world. Paradoxically though, the money was very important to him.

He explained it in this way: *"It's my fuck-off money."* He knew that whatever happened, he'd never have to do anything he didn't want to do, he'd never have to work with anyone he didn't like and he'd never have to do anything against his principles – just to put food on the table. Freedom isn't free it can be pretty expensive, and because of this, being financially secure and strong is very important, even if you have little interest in the material things that money can buy.

Doing Stuff For Nothing Can Make You Money.

Geoff Thompson, who I've mentioned before, told me a fascinating story of how he came to win a BAFTA. He'd written a number of books and was keen to get into film, but just couldn't get any interest. He'd knocked on all the right doors and gone down all the right channels – but all to no avail. For whatever reason, he just couldn't get started.

Anyway, his books were selling well and so he was on a signing tour of bookshops around the UK. At one of these signings a young man, not yet out of his teens, approached him and said he was hoping to get into journalism. Geoff gave him some advice and the young man asked whether he could have an interview for an article that he hoped to sell to a magazine.

Now at this time Geoff was really busy with the tour, but he kept the young man's details and, when he was visiting a town nearby a few weeks later, invited him over for an hour. The young man stayed for most of the day and in between getting information for the interview, pumped Geoff for more help and advice, which he freely gave. No reward was given, and none was asked for. I'm not sure whether that article ever saw the light of day, but here's what did happen.

It turned out that the young man's sister was a film producer. When she heard about Geoff, she contacted him to see whether she could make a documentary about his life. Geoff agreed and she got to know him – and to hear about his other work. It was then that she asked him if he would like to make a short film. Geoff agreed, and set about creating something. The film was called *Bouncer*, and was nominated for a BAFTA. That led to another short film... *Brown Paper Bag*, which won the BAFTA for best short film. And it all came about because he took the time to help someone out, with no immediate promise or chance of recompense or reward.

To make a big success in anything, you have to bypass the employee mindset – the one that demands a fair day's pay for a fair day's work... the one that is constantly trying to match effort with rewards received. You have to move away from demanding an immediate return for your efforts and refusing to do something for nothing. You have to move towards a more holistic lifestyle approach that says effort and reward are rarely in synch, that big rewards will come from the most unlikely sources and, conversely, blood, sweat and tears will often leave you empty-handed.

Geoff's reward did indeed come from a very unlikely source. Big rewards have come from unlikely sources for me too, and it can be the same for you as well. But only if you open yourself up to the possibility. That can only happen when you stop analysing everything you do for its capacity to deliver instant gratification and recompense and start doing things because they just seem like the right things to do.

Thinking Isn't All It's Cracked Up To Be.

Dreams are fascinating. We take them for granted, but if you think about it, they're truly incredible. While you're asleep and unconscious, and not consciously thinking, your brain creates fantastic, detailed and vivid stories all on its own. It creates scenarios and scenes that you couldn't possibly come up with if you were to consciously try. But go to sleep, leave your brain to its own devices and it can do this amazing thing.

If dreams don't convince you of the power of your unconscious mind, then nothing will.

And if it can do that, what else can it do?

Active thinking rarely seems to achieve an awful lot on its own. If I have a problem to solve which requires creative thought, setting aside some time and trying to solve the problem by 'thinking about it' rarely works. Maybe you've found the same thing... the very process of 'thinking' paradoxically seems to preclude creative thought. And the harder you think, the worse the process gets. But totally ignoring the problem doesn't work either!

Perhaps an example would bring this to life, and what better example than this marvellous book. (I've been thinking about becoming more modest, but was doing it actively, so it didn't really work.) Anyway, let's say I decide that I want to write a book, but don't know what to write about. What should I do?

Well, one solution could be to sit down and have a good think about it. I could set aside an hour, go somewhere quiet and actively think through the problem of what to write about. And I'd almost certainly come up with nothing. The other obvious solution is to ignore the problem completely and hope it solves itself, that a solution will appear, that my subconscious mind will create something useful. It might… but I might not live that long, and neither might you! Fortunately there's a better way.

You rarely reach a creative solution to a problem by thinking it through to a conclusion and you rarely reach a successful creative solution by leaving your mind to its own devices. Why? Because it needs something to work with.

Dreams are fantastic things, but they're pretty useless in the real world. There's no focus to them. Your subconscious mind seems to fairly randomly select events, people and thoughts from your recent and past history, jumbles them up, and then uses them to create a story. If your dreams are anything like mine, these stories are never rational or cohesive. They have no useful message, and they do nothing to solve an apparent problem. That's because they're 'fed' randomly. There's no focus to the material that goes into creating them, so there's no focus to the narrative that comes out. If you want your subconscious mind to come up with something useful, you have to feed it the right material.

In practical terms, this means that, rather than sitting down and trying to come up with a creative solution, you should sit down and bring together all the background material and information you have surrounding the problem you're trying to solve. And then you do nothing. Going back to the book writing example, that could mean reviewing all the interesting pieces I've torn out of newspapers over the last week, all the items I've photocopied from books, and then jotting down details of any interesting conversations or experiences I've had over the last week or so.

And then doing nothing!

And more often than not, within a few minutes of waking up one morning over the next day or so... while laying there daydreaming and staring into space... I'll have an idea for a book or a newsletter. And within 10 minutes or so, I'll have it almost completely written in my head. While I've been asleep, my subconscious mind has been working on the material I've given it to work with and created a solution.

Now I know this all sounds a bit madcap... a bit fanciful... but you already know that unfocused thoughts, events and ideas are turned into unfocused dreams by the subconscious mind. Is it too much of a leap to believe that focused inputs can be converted into focused outputs via the same subconscious route?

The subconscious, however, sets its own pace to work to, and there's no telling when it will spew out its conclusions. Early morning is a key time because you're relaxed, and the subconscious has had all night to do its work. It's also a time when most people are in a rush, harassed and not very receptive to new ideas and thoughts. If you're the sort of person who gets woken by an alarm clock, jumps straight out of bed and gets on with the practical issues of the day, then you're going to miss this key time altogether... and any insights and ideas it might bring. So you need to set aside some time in the day for doing absolutely nothing. The first half hour in a morning on waking is ideal, but if you can't manage that, you need to set aside quiet time with no distractions at some other point in the day.

Most successful people are very aware of the power and importance of this process, which is why if you're ever criticised for slothfulness, you can be sure that the criticism will be coming from someone who's never achieved an awful lot. I'll leave you with a story about Henry Ford that illustrates perfectly what I've been trying to get over.

Ford contracted a firm of time and motion specialists to take a look at part of his operation and report back. They asked Ford to accompany them on a tour of his offices and they stopped at one point where a young man was sitting with his feet up on the desk staring into space. *"See him,"* said the time and motion man, *"we've been past here a dozen times in the past week and he's always got his feet up on the desk doing nothing. You should fire him."*

"Well that's interesting," said Ford. *"You see, 12 months ago, that man had an idea that saved us $2 million, and when he had that idea he was sitting in exactly the same position you see him in now. One day, I reckon he'll have another idea like that, and I'd hate to miss it."*

You've no idea how many times I've had to tell that story!

Specialists Take The Spoils.

Albert Einstein was walking through the park near Princeton University when he met up with a work colleague. They chatted for 15 minutes or so, and as they were ready to part, Einstein asked a question. *"When we stopped here,"* he said, *"which way was I walking – towards my house or away from my house?"*

"Away from your house," answered the bemused colleague. *"Ah good,"* said Einstein. *"That means I've had my lunch."*

Now here was the most accomplished and revered scientist of the 20th Century… a man who most people instantly bring to mind when the word 'genius' is used. And yet not only could he not remember which way he'd been walking just a few minutes earlier, but he also didn't know whether he'd eaten!

Einstein is not alone, because many successful people in one field are absolutely hopeless to the point of dysfunction in others. They do one thing exceptionally well, but are almost abnormally poor in other areas. There's a term that is often used these days to describe people like this. And it's a term that is always used disparagingly. That term is: 'one trick pony'.

Now here's what's interesting. Society, competition, business and sport… just about everything you can think of favours and rewards one trick ponies. It favours people who do just one thing abnormally well. And what's more, this is a growing trend. Take the Olympic Games for example.

The days of amateur competition are long gone, and there are massive rewards at stake for anyone who can win a gold medal. The difference in financial reward between gold and silver is surprisingly large. And the people who win those gold medals will do one thing brilliantly, but would be laughed out of the stadium if they tried to compete in another event. The winner of the men's 100 metres would struggle to even finish the 5,000 metres, let alone come in the top three. He has trained and prepared his body for just 10 seconds of explosive action to the exclusion of everything else. Conversely, the winner of the marathon, who finishes the 26-mile course looking fresh as a daisy, would finish the 100 metres just a crumpled heap on the track... in last. He has prepared his body for endurance, not speed. Nearly all of the 302 Olympic competitions don't favour the 'jacks of all trades', they favour the 'masters of one'.

It's the same in any sport. To rise to the top in soccer, you want to be the best striker... not a good striker who can defend a bit. The number one striker will earn many times the rewards of the fifth-best, even if the fifth-best is also a good defender. It's almost inconceivable that anyone could possess the multiple talents to be the 10th-best golfer in the world and the 10th-best tennis player. But even if they could, they'd be far better rewarded if they were the best in one of those sports, rather than the 10th-best in both.

The big rewards always go to those at the top and fall away disproportionally once you descend, even a short way, from the peak.

So what's all this got to do with you? Well if you're to be successful in life, you really need to work towards being the best at one thing, rather than 'good' at a lot of things. The 'best' are rewarded disproportionally, even though the tangible gap between them and the rest may be small. So you need to specialise... and then you need to stop worrying about what you can't do. Because if you get really good at the thing you specialise in, you'll easily be able to afford to pay people to do the things you're bad at.

Einstein didn't become such a great scientist by cluttering his mind with the mundane things he needed to do each day. Usain Bolt didn't become a great sprinter by simultaneously trying to become a professional footballer. And you won't rise to the top in your field by trying to be a competent all-rounder. Because if you try to do that, while you'll probably be better at most things than most people, there will always be somebody who is better at everything you do. And those people will always get the largest slice of the pie.

I don't, however, want to mislead you with all this talk of world-famous scientists and sportsmen. I don't operate on that level, and you probably don't either. Very few of us can ever be 'the best' in the way that Einstein was the best, or a multi-Olympic gold medallist like Usain Bolt is the best. But within our own niche... within your own world, we can be. You can become the best there is at what you do in the arena in which you compete. That might not be the world stage, but that doesn't really matter because the principle is exactly the same. The bulk of the spoils go to the specialist 'master' not the generalist 'jack'.

First Offers Are Never The Best Offers.

I bought a house recently. Nothing particularly unusual in that. Over the past few years I've bought about seventy properties and still have most of them. But this one has caused me more mental torment than most. I should explain that I have a property business and all these properties – a mixture of houses, flats and commercial units – are let out to tenants.

But this was different. It was a property I bought for personal use and, because of that, some of the decisions about the purchase weren't solely in my hands. My wife wanted the house and would have been 'disappointed' if I didn't secure it. Anyway, I was motivated to complete a deal on the house, but I was also conscious of the need to pay the right price. My normal tactic of offering a price equal to the value of a two-bed terrace in Darlington circa 1984 was not going to wash. So I came up with an offer that was challenging, but not insulting. What happened next is the source of my mental torment… the offer was accepted!

Just like that. No haggling, no time taken to think about it, no if, buts or maybes – just a quick acceptance of the offer. Arm duly snapped off.

Now what do you think my reaction was when that happened? What would your reaction be? If your brain were wired up like most of us, you'd probably think one of two things – and probably both in quick succession:

1. I offered too much. I could have got it cheaper.
2. Perhaps there's something wrong with it.

In the case of a property, the second thought can be dispensed with pretty easily via a survey and some due diligence on the area, neighbours and neighbourhood. But the first thought will stay with you for all time.

Negotiation is a massive subject, and not one I'm particularly skilled or knowledgeable in, but I do know this – if you accept the first offer made, you're doing neither party any favours. You won't get the maximum amount for what you're selling and the buyer will go away with the nagging feeling that he's overpaid.

In any negotiation, you're looking to achieve a win-win situation – both buyer and seller getting what they want from the deal. By accepting the first offer, you're doing just the opposite. You're making the buyer feel uncomfortable and potentially throwing money away at the same time.

Paradoxically, being asked to pay a few thousand more would have reduced my mental torment! How counter-intuitive and illogical is that? And yet if you put yourself in the same position, I think you'd probably feel the same way.

Would I have actually paid any more? We'll never know, because nobody tried to find out – maybe not. But at least everyone would feel more comfortable. The seller would know that the limit had been reached and I'd know (or at least be made to think!) that my offer was right on the wire.

Whenever you're negotiating anything, I'd urge you to keep this firmly in mind. You'll get a better deal for yourself and send the other party away happier (if a little poorer) for the experience.

Nobody Thinks They're To Blame.
Don't Disillusion Them.

Probably the best self-help book ever written is *How To Win Friends And Influence People* by Dale Carnegie. It was the forerunner to so many other books, courses and audio programmes and, although the language used now seems a little archaic, its underlying messages are as relevant today as they ever were. If you haven't read it, do it now. You won't be disappointed.

Anyway, one of the quotations that always sticks in my mind from the book, comes from Al Capone (that gives you some idea how long ago it was written) when he says: *"I have spent the best years of my life giving people the lighter pleasures, helping them have a good time, and all I get is abuse, the existence of a hunted man."*

Yes that's the notorious Chicago gangster Al Capone – the man responsible for more murder and mayhem than anyone else in his era. And yet he didn't condemn or blame himself for anything. In fact he saw himself as a public benefactor – somebody doing good for his fellow man and not being appreciated for it – someone wronged and misunderstood. To a greater or lesser extent, most of us are like Al Capone. We have a high capacity for self-justification and are remarkably resistant to evidence or persuasion that we are wrong, or in some way to blame for events.

You may have noticed that I use a fair amount of ink in this book, attempting to dissuade you from one set of life choices and move you towards another. In the course of that I'm obliquely being critical of what you're presently doing and laying the blame (if indeed there's anything for you to be blamed for) right at your door. Now I know you're resistant to any suggestions I might make and I also know you're defensive in the face of criticism. But it's for your own good, for goodness sake. And that's why I do it. But... and here's the thing.

If I were trying to sell you something, wanted you to like me or treat me favourably, it would be foolish of me to point out your shortcomings, your failings and your errors. It would be silly of me to point out that in all likelihood, if you have problems that need solutions, it's your own fault. You're to blame. Why? Because you'd reject my criticism, as well as rejecting both what I'm offering and me at the same time.

The people you interact with each day don't believe they are to blame for anything, so why antagonise them by suggesting that they are? They believe they've been misunderstood, unlucky, misinformed, exploited, conned, tricked and misled in the past. They take comfort in the fact that it wasn't their fault. So why swim against the tide? Pointing out why they're wrong and to blame will only move what you want from the relationship all the further away.

Momentum Brings the Biggest Rewards.

Like a lot of cars these days, mine has a fancy computer in it that tells me all sorts of useful information I never wanted to know. One of the most disconcerting settings is the one that delivers an instant reading of the fuel consumption. Accelerate at anything above Reliant-Robin-with-the-handbrake-on pace, and the digital read-out falls rapidly into single figures. It takes a surprising amount of energy (fuel) to take the car from standstill to a reasonable speed.

But when you reach cruising speed, the read-out is equally surprising. The energy required to keep the car at 70mph is less than half that required to take it from 20mph to 30mph. The fuel-sapping part is the take-off and acceleration. Speed, in itself, does not require great amounts of energy to maintain. Why? Because of the build up of momentum.

It's all got something to do with Newton's laws of motion – a subject with which I would be delighted to bore you at length, had I paid a little more attention in physics at school. No matter, you don't need to understand the science to appreciate the concept. You see the role of momentum isn't confined to the world of physics. It plays a huge part on the road to attainment and achievement.

To make a standing start takes a great deal of effort at the outset. Just as the computer on my car shows a huge amount of fuel being gobbled up while getting up to cruising speed, precisely the same effort-to-reward ratio is present in the early days of any endeavour. We put in a huge effort, and seem to get disproportionately little in return at the start. And it's for exactly the same reason – we have yet to build momentum.

Once momentum builds, we get the same benefits as we do in our cars. The ratio between effort and reward shifts in our favour. We put in just a little more effort, and get a disproportionately high reward for it. We're not expending nearly so much energy and yet the benefits we derive are so much greater.

In the early stages of working towards a goal, it will probably seem like the rewards you're getting don't justify the tremendous effort you're putting in. At times, you'll maybe look at friends and relatives who are striving for nothing in particular and envy them. Stay with it! In a relatively short time, you'll have momentum working in your favour rather than against you. That's the power of momentum and it's well worth sticking around for.

Saving Money Is Fine
But Making Money Is Better.

It's far better to put effort into making money than it is to put effort into saving it, but far fewer people do it. People, who would happily get up at 4.00am to stand in a queue for the Next sale, wouldn't lift a finger to boost their income. And that's just plain silly.

You see, when you invest time seeking out bargains, your savings are finite. They're limited to a percentage of what you intend to spend. But when you invest time in making money, your gains are limitless. They're not restricted to a percentage of what you spend, to the total amount you spend, or even to the amount you could ever dream of spending in your lifetime. That's the exciting thing. There's no limit at all.

The bottom line is that when you're deciding where to expend effort in a quest to improve your financial position, you need to bear this relationship in mind. That doesn't mean you shouldn't attempt to save money where you can, but it does mean you should be realistic about the relative impact of saving money and making money on your lifestyle.

Burning Your Bridges Is Always Dumb.

Over the years, you will enter into relationships with many different people and organisations. A lot of these will be transient and not particularly satisfactory. You may already have had relationships that you have no desire to continue. When these relationships are particularly bad, there is an inevitable temptation to end them with a flourish that ensures there's no going back. This is usually a very bad idea.

Dave Dickhead who was your boss at your first part-time job may well have lived up to his name. When you left, you might have taken great satisfaction in telling him exactly what you thought of him. But that satisfaction may come at a price when five years down the road you have gone into the widget business and Dave has got a new job as chief widget buyer for Mega Enterprises. This may seem far-fetched but you will be astounded by how often you cross paths with people you thought were out of your life for good.

There's an old saying that you should be nice to people on the way up because you'll meet them again on the way down. I'm not sure about the 'up and down' business, but it's certainly true that people and organisations will regularly become significant to you again, long after you think you've seen the back of them. You have no way of knowing which people or organisations these will be or when it will happen. So keep as many doors open, and as many bridges intact, as possible. In practical terms, that means parting on the best possible terms with everyone – employers, employees, workmates, bosses, friends, colleagues, lovers, spouses – even if the relationship has become strained or broken. The perfect scenario is one where you feel able to re-establish contact but with no obligation to do so.

There Are Many Routes To The Same Destination.

When musician Moby released the album *Play*, in 1999, it was a critical disaster. Just 30 people turned up to the launch party, and the omens weren't good. So how come it went on to sell over 10 million copies? The answer is fascinating, and contains within it, one of the major keys to success in anything.

The 'normal' way to make money from a record (certainly in pre-Internet days) is to get it played as much as possible on the radio and TV. People hear it, like it and go out and buy the album. And then the bandwagon starts to gather pace. But, with thousands of artists battling for a limited amount of airtime, it isn't easy for a relative unknown to get significant coverage. Without radio and TV coverage nobody gets to hear the music. And if they don't hear it, they don't go out and buy it. At first, nobody was playing *Play*, and nobody was buying it.

The record company (and Moby himself, who was broke at the time) were keen to recoup some money from what was looking like a disaster. What they did was probably done as a last resort, but it turned the record into a hit and Moby into a star.

They started licensing the tracks on the album for use in advertising campaigns. I don't know whether they did it purely for the licencing fees, or whether they had the longer game in mind from the start, but the outcome was that the songs on the album quickly gained a massive audience… far bigger than could normally be achieved from radio play alone. *Play* was the first album to have all its tracks licensed for use in either advertising or films. People heard the songs in the ads and movies, liked them, and went out and bought the album. The rest is history.

The point is this — there's always more than one route to the same destination... in this case a multi-million, best-selling record. Your destination will probably be different, but there will still be numerous routes to get there.

There will be the well-trodden path that everyone else is on. It will be crowded and uncomfortable and you're going to have a real fight on your hands to make any progress. In music terms, think about the huge queue of 'hopefuls' outside the *X Factor* auditions and you get the idea. And then there will be other paths, which may take a little lateral thinking to reach, but they'll be less crowded and you'll get the chance to do things on your own terms. Compare the rise of Arctic Monkeys via the Internet and word of mouth to that of your average *X Factor* winner, and you'll see what I mean.

It's difficult for me to be specific here, because I don't know what you're involved in, or working on, but the principle is this: whatever you're aiming to achieve, there are back roads, shortcuts and alternative routes away from the main highway that everyone else is using. Once you separate yourself from the crowd, the rules of the road are far more flexible. You get to do things your way... maybe even carve out a piece of your own track while nobody's looking.

It's all the more satisfying when you arrive at your destination, knowing that you've done it on your terms and avoided becoming a physical or emotional casualty of the mainstream journey.

You Have Hidden Skills...
So Look For Them.

In my mid-forties I started ice-skating again after a gap of over 30 years. Rather surprisingly I was quickly up to my old standard – and then I actually improved!

When I skated as a kid, I never got beyond going forwards, but when I started again, I decided I wanted to learn to go backwards. I thought it looked really impressive, and so resolved to learn how to do it, which I did. It's a great feeling to learn something new, but here's the interesting thing: as soon as I could do it, it wasn't impressive any more.

I remember exactly the same feeling when I learned to juggle, to ski, to memorise a pack of playing cards... and loads of other stuff. They all seemed impossibly impressive skills when I couldn't do them, but pretty mundane once I could. I find this holds true with most things in life, and I suspect it's the same for you.

Now, of course I'm talking about 'fun' activities here, but this has wider implications because it lures us in to undervaluing all the skills we have – to regard them as something anyone can do. And the longer we've had those skills, the more likely we are to undervalue them – the more likely we are to feel that it's commonplace and worthless. Indeed we might have even stopped recognising them as skills at all.

I spend quite a bit of time writing stuff... books, newsletters, sales letters, advertisements etc... but rarely do I regard it as a skill. I just think it's something that anyone can do... like talking. Of course, when I think about it – or sometimes when I see someone else trying to do the same thing – I realise that it's not as easy as I think; that there is a skill to it.

I'd wager it's the same for you. There are things you do very well, but undervalue because you simply don't think of it as a rare skill. As a result, you undervalue it or don't do enough of it. You see, to maximise your productivity and income, you need to be capitalising on your most rare and most valuable skills. That's where your greatest commercial value lies.

So here's my suggestion for you. Make a dispassionate and objective list of your skills and analyse whether you're exploiting them to the fullest. I wouldn't be surprised if you quickly find a hidden gem waiting to be mined, cut and polished.

Spending To Impress Is Stupid.

Pay heed to just this one thing, and it will repay the price of this book at least a thousand times over. Maybe more.

Left to your own devices, you will waste huge chunks of time and effort attempting to gain the approval of people who have no influence or impact on your life, and money is one tool you will use to do it. Think about this for a moment: why do you feel the need to impress other people, and if you do feel the need, why do you think you can do it by spending money?

So someone likes the car, house, clothes or possessions that you own, but can't really afford them. Or maybe they don't like them. How does that impact on your life either way? Plainly it doesn't, unless you decide that it does. They are not going to shower you with love, money or adoration because of the trinkets you've accumulated.

Does that mean you should never bother having 'nice things'? Absolutely not, but get them on your own terms. Only buy stuff because it genuinely pleases you… and when you can afford to do it. Follow this simple philosophy and you will save a substantial fortune over your lifetime.

Many people go broke seeking the approval and admiration of others via their credit card or overdraft. Not only is it futile and self-defeating, but also it doesn't have the desired effect. What do you think of people who try to impress others with their possessions and apparent wealth? That's right, you think they're a jerk! Why would you want to appear to be one of those?

The News Is Cerebral Sabotage.

In his book, *Thinking, Fast and Slow*, Nobel prize-winning author Daniel Kahneman writes about a fascinating experiment carried out at New York University by psychologist, John Bargh.

A group of 18- to 22-year-old students were selected at random and asked to create a sentence from four words (such as 'finds, he, yellow, instantly' for example). For half the group, words loosely associated with old age were included in the selection – words like 'grey, wrinkle, bald and Florida'. The other half had a different set of words without this association. When they'd completed the exercise, they were asked to go to another classroom, where there would be other tests to do.

The researchers then sat down to analyse the data they'd collected, but they didn't even look at the papers filled out by the students. You see the exercise wasn't really part of the experiment at all. What the researchers were really interested in was the speed at which the students travelled from one classroom to the other. Unbeknown to them, the researchers were measuring the speed at which the two groups of students walked, and what they discovered was truly remarkable.

Those students exposed to words that are obliquely associated with old age acted as if they were older themselves. They walked significantly slower than the group exposed to a more neutral selection of words. Remember the words used: 'grey, wrinkle, bald and Florida'. There was nothing overtly elderly implied such as 'old, arthritis, crippled or disabled'. The students weren't asked to imagine what it would be like to be old and infirm. Old age wasn't mentioned at all. And yet mere exposure to words, which might be subconsciously linked to the ageing process, caused them to walk slower. When questioned later, none of the students reported noticing the theme in the words, and none considered that this theme could have impacted on their subsequent behaviour. Isn't that astonishing?

As I write this, the Olympic Games in London has just come to an end and I'm sad. Not only because it was a fantastic sporting spectacle, but also because for two solid weeks it was as if bad news had suddenly stopped happening. News programmes were dominated by Olympic triumphs and newspapers devoted page after page to medal-winning success. If there was bad stuff happening, we didn't really get to hear about it. What an incredible breath of fresh air.

For most of the year though, the media is not really interested in good news at all. What it is interested in is attracting readers and viewers, and for reasons I can't even begin to comprehend, research shows that people tend to gravitate towards bad news. Economic crises, unemployment, war, famine, health scares, extreme weather, natural disasters, crime, violence, riots... they're all events to be spotlighted and magnified by the media in its quest for more readers and viewers. Meanwhile every day, a huge amount of positive and exciting news either goes unreported or doesn't get nearly the coverage it deserves. And this matters. It matters a lot.

If we go back to John Bargh's experiment, look what happened when people were exposed to words and thoughts even slightly suggestive of something potentially negative such as old age. They acted as though they were physically affected by the negative implications of old age themselves, even though they weren't. They started to walk more slowly, but weren't aware of it and certainly wouldn't have been able to tell you why. The effect was probably short-lived, but the stimulus was both weak and brief.

Now imagine for a moment, the impact of a constant and unrelenting bombardment of bad news and negativity courtesy of the media. This isn't some lightweight, subtle and short-term exposure to a few words that might be loosely associated with something negative – it's a full-blown heavy assault. Everything is crap, and you're stuck right in the middle of it. How do you think we react to that – even without consciously thinking about it?

We are told that things are bad and guess what happens – we act as though things are bad! We start to 'walk' more slowly, and the worse we're told things are, the slower we 'walk'. And pretty soon, everyone gives in and starts walking slowly as well. You can apply this to whatever piece of bad news you like, but in economic terms, we're told that everyone is becoming poorer and so we feel poorer too. We start to act as if we are poorer by spending less money. We adopt a poverty mentality. Others see us doing this and decide that they must be poorer as well and cut their spending. Pretty soon we're all poorer and have less money to spend. It all becomes so depressingly self-fulfilling.

Those Olympic athletes I mentioned earlier put a great deal of time, effort and research into ensuring that they are fuelled by the right nutrients; so they steer clear of the sort of junk that pollutes their body and blunts their performance. Those of us whose successful outcomes rely more upon the cerebral than the physical should be no less vigilant. It's quite clear that the psychological 'food' we consume will have a massive impact on our thoughts, actions and the results we ultimately achieve.

We can't extend the Olympic Games indefinitely, but we can stop watching the TV news and reading the newspapers. If World War III is declared, a comet is set to destroy the earth, or the pound is devalued to parity with the Zimbabwean dollar you'll get to hear about it soon enough. Pretty much everything else you can live without and be a lot happier, healthier and more effective for not being exposed to it.

Showing Love And Appreciation Is Complicated!

On the face of it, this should be straightforward. We know from countless studies that everyone wants to feel loved and appreciated. Demonstrate to those around us that we love and/or appreciate them (where each is appropriate!) and the results can only be positive for everyone. Unfortunately, it's not that simple.

Difficulty arises here because we tend to assume that showing love and appreciation has a universal meaning. This isn't the case. For example, in personal relationships, there are five different ways of showing love, and obviously by definition, receiving love. These are kind words, kind deeds, gifts, physical affection and spending some quality time. Problems can occur in a relationship when the parties' needs are not compatible... when one partner's natural pattern of behaviour is to show love in ways that the other partner doesn't readily appreciate.

It may be, for example, that one party enjoys receiving presents. They think their partner will feel the same way, so shower him or her with gifts. But the partner isn't receptive to this at all. You see, in the past, they've been in relationships with people who have used gifts as a substitute for attention (or maybe as an apology) and therefore to them, the giving of presents has a negative connotation.

Or it may be that one party likes to hear kind, loving words from the other, and so expresses love in that way. However, they may not get the expected response because in past relationships, kind words have been used as a precursor to the delivery of unpleasant news, an unreasonable request or as a set up for an insult or put-down. The words create discomfort – maybe even on a subliminal level – when their intention is quite the opposite.

There's a lot more to it, but hopefully you get the idea – that two people can interpret seemingly positive words, gestures and actions in completely different ways – so different in fact, that it creates conflict. Why? Because, the reaction of one party can be so radically opposed to what the other expects. It's a fairly small step to realise that if this is true for personal relationships, it's true for all relationships – including business and workplace ones.

Now I'm not suggesting for a moment that you want to express love for your business or work colleagues – or indeed that physical affection and spending quality time together would be appropriate ways of doing it – but I am suggesting that you need to think carefully about how you express and demonstrate appreciation to them.

Whoever you're dealing with – partners, friends, colleagues or business associates, take some time to find out the type of person they are, and what sort of appreciation would receive the best reception from them. In most communications, the best approach (and certainly the one to use in the absence of other information) is 'treat others as you'd like to be treated yourself'. There are times, however, when this clearly doesn't work as you might expect.

Nobody Needs To Get Fat!

There's a myth that gaining weight (or body fat to be more precise) is an inevitable part of growing older. Certainly if you see people who are five, ten or twenty years older than you, the evidence before your eyes would suggest a progression.

While it's certainly true that metabolism can slow down with age (usually starting in the mid- to late-20s) and this makes it easier to gain weight, it's far from inevitable or a done deal. If you think about it, that makes about as much sense as believing it's inevitable that you will get colder if the temperature drops. You won't of course, because you will take action. Perhaps you'll turn the heating up or put some more clothes on or maybe jump up and down if the other options aren't open to you. What you won't do is stand there and say: *"the temperature's dropping so I suppose I'm going to get colder."*

Avoiding unwanted weight gain is exactly the same. If your metabolism slows, you take action. Put very simply, that means you eat less or move around more. The only reason you would gain weight with age is if you ignore what's happening to your body.

Diets Don't Work.

When I was growing up, there was only one product marketed as a 'diet food' as far as I can remember. That was Nimble bread. If you were sitting here with me now, and I was feeling particularly acrimonious towards you, I could sing you the TV ad all the way through. Fast-forward over 30 years and there are hundreds (if not thousands) of diet-related foods, potions, drinks and tablets on offer. And guess what? We're all fatter than ever!

Hardly an evening's TV passes these days without a programme hosted by a celebrity chef or media-whore doctor telling fat people that they are in fact, fat and it's not good for them. Now you might think this is a pointless exercise – that they are telling them something they already know – but you'd be surprised. Or at least I am.

As the truth is revealed to them – *"You're a bloater and you'll probably die early,"* (they dress it up a bit, but that is the gist) – you can see the shock on their faces. Of course, the experts are on hand to put a reassuring arm around their shoulder and tell them that it isn't too late to change. But I suspect their real reaction is more akin to mine as I yell at the TV set (a sure sign of madness): *"Don't you have any bloody mirrors where you come from? You must have known you were a space-hopper smuggler before you came on the programme!"*

When I was at school, the fat kids could be counted on the fingers of one hand. They had a torrid time and I'd imagine have carried the scars of PE lesson humiliation well into later life. At least, the fatties aren't so isolated these days – they've got plenty of company. It doesn't take a genius to work out that something doesn't quite add up here, and a great deal of time, money and effort has been spent trying to find out what.

Because nobody is ever to blame for anything anymore, a lot has been made of the role of a so-called 'fat gene'. The fat gene is great news for the overweight because they can carry on eating, secure in the knowledge that their resemblance to Michelin man's portlier brother is beyond their control. Sadly though, this is something of a red herring. If there is such a thing as a fat gene, it existed when Nimble was flavour of the month and we were all relatively slim. That's the thing about genes... they're passed from generation to generation. I'm no scientist, but I know that much. If there's a fat gene now, there had to be a fat gene then. And we weren't fat!

The obvious conclusion is that we're getting fatter because, of something we're doing, not because of a gene. In other words – steel yourself, you might not be able to comprehend what I'm saying – we have to take responsibility for our own blubbery bodies.

Well, we do up to a point. You see the combination of confusing (and conflicting) advice from experts, together with the burgeoning output from a multi-billion pound processed food industry has rendered most of us unsure about what we should be eating and uncertain of the nutritional value of what we're being sold.

With that in mind, here are three very simple rules, which, if you live by, will probably negate the need for dieting.

1. Eat food, but stop before you're full.
2. Don't eat anything your grandmother wouldn't recognise as food.
3. Avoid products made from ingredients you can't pronounce.

I can't resist adding one more piece of advice from Billy Connolly of all people... *"Never eat anything that comes in a bucket!"*

I reckon if we all made a stab at following those basic rules, the obesity epidemic would be all but over. And the diet gurus would be forced to drag their scrawny arses (as you see I'm completely non-discriminatory in my insults) down to the job centre.

Getting Fat Once Has Lifelong Implications.

Don't get fat! I think I need to clarify this – you might be happy carrying extra weight. Don't ever get any heavier or fatter than you're personally comfortable with. Gaining weight is easy to do – particularly after your mid-twenties – and the common perception is that it's no big deal. It's something that won't harm your health in the short term and can be rectified later in life when it might become more of a problem. This is a big mistake.

When you gain weight, fat cells become activated, and unfortunately they have a memory. So once you've activated a fat cell, you can't reverse that process. Yes, you can lose weight and fat from the cell, but once activated, the cell will forever be prone to filling up again. Imagine it a bit like a balloon. Filling it with air the first time is hard, but let the air out and try again and it's far easier to inflate second time around. That's one of the reasons why people who have been overweight have a tough time keeping the weight off – their bodies internal fat memory is working overtime. This doesn't mean you can never lose weight if you've allowed yourself to get fat, but maintaining the improvement will be more difficult and require more self-discipline than for someone who has always stayed in reasonable physical shape.

The good news is that muscles have memory too, and if you've got in shape once, it will be much easier to do it the second time around. Get muscle and fat memory working in your favour, and the constant dieting and sacrifice, which characterises the lives of many after the age of thirty, will be something for others to worry about. You need to start taking action now though.

Cutting Out The Foods
You Love Will Never Work.

If you're going to maintain a healthy weight throughout the rest of your life, it's important that you eat what you like. Deny yourself nothing. This may seem counter-intuitive and contrary to what you've been told, but there are a couple of important provisos. The first is that you can't eat *only* what you like, and the second is that you can't eat too much of it. If you enjoy eating chocolate, stodgy puddings, crisps, fish and chips or whatever other supposedly 'banned' foods take your fancy, then you should do it. But just don't do it all the time, and when you do, keep the portion sizes down.

Restricted diets rarely, if ever, work over time. Denying yourself your favourite foods may have a positive short-term effect – on your weight, if not your mood – but eventually the pressure will build and you'll crack. And when you do, it will be as if a dam has burst. All-or-nothing behaviour like this has only one long-term outcome – an ever-increasing bodyweight and an ever-steeper mountain to climb.

So eat the stuff you know that's good for you... I'm sure you know what that is... but don't give up the foods you really like. You'll be a great deal leaner, healthier and, more importantly, happier, as a result.

Weighing Yourself Daily Will Help Keep You Slim.

A large proportion of the population are unhappy with their body weight after the age of thirty, and the problem is now becoming more common further down the age range. Get weighed every day: do this and you will prevent a small problem developing into a big one. This rule applies whether you want to lose weight, gain weight or stay the same.

Conventional advice is that you should get weighed rarely, or indeed not get weighed at all, using the mirror instead to monitor progress. The argument runs that body weight can fluctuate on a daily basis and it's not the most important determinant of your condition. Muscle weighs heavier than fat. It's what you look like that's important. I'm sure you've heard these arguments before. None hold water.

Whatever you're trying to achieve, it's important that you get feedback and the more regular and accurate, the better. If you're on a journey of any kind, the sooner you realise you've taken a wrong turn the better. Otherwise you're just further down the wrong track when you are alerted to the need to take action. The scales will tell you long before a mirror what is happening to your body. Yes, weight can fluctuate from one day to the next, but if you get weighed just once a week, month or fortnight, you could just as easily hit an atypical day. When you weigh yourself every day, you quickly iron out any short-term discrepancies and realise what your 'real' weight is.

The bathroom scales shouldn't be your only tool for assessing your condition, but it should be your first port of call each day. After that you can use the mirror, a tape or the fit of your clothes to determine the true nature of any changes.

Get weighed each morning and there's no hiding from what's happening. It will re-focus you on what you need to do to achieve your weight management goals during that day. The sooner you start taking action to correct your course, the quicker you'll get on track and the less painful the action will be.

Knowing The 'Price' Of Everything You Eat Can Control Your Weight.

When you go into a clothes shop, what stops you buying everything you like? That's right, it's the price. You look at the labels, figure out how much you can afford to spend and then select the things you like most within your budget. Am I right? Well I'm suggesting you do exactly the same thing with your food – but the price isn't a monetary one.

I've owned a rowing machine for many years now and its apparent effect on the passage of time is quite extraordinary. Flop into your favourite armchair to watch a TV programme, and half an hour passes before you know it, but set the timer to 30 minutes on the rowing machine and it's like time is standing still. If you could somehow recreate that effect across your whole life, you'd live to about 297! Or at least it would feel like it. And it has another strange effect too, because it helped me discover a foolproof method of weight control.

You see the rower has a computer, which measures the calories burned during exercise. I know for example, that I burn about 400 calories in half an hour. Remember, this isn't a regular half an hour. It's a rowing machine half an hour, which is a lot longer. So when I look at the label on a cream cake, and see there are 425 calories in it, you can bet your life that I'm going to think very carefully about whether I really want it, because I know 'the price'. More than half an hour's hard labour on that damned machine.

Just as you might compare the price of two pairs of jeans, I do exactly the same thing with two different ready-made sandwiches... the tuna mayonnaise costs me 22 minutes while the BLT costs me 47. No contest. Calorie numbers are meaningless unless you equate them to something tangible. Learn the real price of your food and it will help immeasurably with weight control.

Exercise Is Good. But Not Too Much!

When I was growing up, anyone who exercised at all was seen as a bit strange and anyone who exercised over the age of 30 was a complete fruitcake. You could play football of course, in fact you could play football until you were a hundred, but that wasn't exercise; it was a game. It's only over the last 25 years or so that exercising for your health has taken hold as a concept. Nowadays, it isn't unusual to see people of all ages exercising in an attempt to control their weight, keep healthy and improve their appearance. Is this an example you should follow?

Well the physical and psychological benefits of exercise are well documented. In short, you'll look better and feel better if you exercise regularly. What's more, you'll find it easier and more beneficial if you start sooner rather than later. Establishing and maintaining good exercise habits is a lot easier when you're young. The older you are, the less successful you're likely to be.

It's well established that there are three elements to physical fitness – cardiovascular fitness, strength and flexibility. And a well-rounded exercise programme should cover all three. Many people become obsessed with just one of the three, leading to benefits that are less than optimal. What's more, too much of a good thing can actually be harmful.

Doing a large amount of high-impact exercise like running for example, while good for the cardiovascular system, has a negative impact on joints and connective tissue over time. It's generally agreed that low-impact activities, like swimming, cycling and rowing, while offering similar cardiovascular benefits, are a far safer alternative if you want to avoid debilitating conditions like arthritis in later life.

During my youth, resistance training using weights was regarded as an activity reserved for narcissists and weirdos. I did it anyway, which may tell you something! Over the past quarter century opinions have changed markedly, with health-conscious people of both sexes starting to recognise the aesthetic, health and practical benefits of gaining and maintaining strength. Again though, there can be issues. Using too much weight can lead to joint and connective tissue problems that can negate some of the benefits in the long run. There's no substitute for a sensible strength/weight-training programme though, particularly if aesthetics are important to you. Running won't make you look better, (just look at the people pounding the streets!) but weight training will.

The third piece in the jigsaw is flexibility. You don't have to go back too far to find a time when yoga was the exclusive preserve of women, and pretty strange ones at that. Today, many top sports people use it as part of their programme and footballer Ryan Giggs attributed his longevity in the game to yoga as he approached his 40th year and 22nd season in the top flight. It helps flexibility, which in turn helps prevent injuries. There are a number of stretching, flexibility and yoga-type practices to choose from. Find something that suits.

Your lifetime exercise requirements need be no more complicated than that. Set aside 20 minutes to half an hour a day, research and choose activities based on cardiovascular fitness, strength and flexibility and do them in rotation. If you can find stuff you enjoy doing in each category, so much the better. If you can't, just do something! Keep impact-based activities to a minimum, keep resistance training within sensible bounds, stay flexible and you'll reap lifelong benefits while avoiding the pitfalls of over-exercising.

You CAN Find The Time.

Throughout your life, there will be things you know you should be doing but won't do them because you 'don't have the time'. This can apply to anything, but we just talked about exercise, so let's stick with that by way of example. Lack of time is the number one excuse people use for not exercising. It's just that, an excuse. Here's how to overcome it.

So you can't figure out how to fit exercise into your day? No problem. You don't complain that you can't fit in work or sleeping or eating, so why should exercise be any different? It's simply a state of mind. You hardwire exercise into your daily routine at a time that suits you and that's it – fixed. No need to think about fitting it in because it's already there – first. Perhaps you then need to think about how you might fit in less important activities like watching TV, surfing the Internet, socialising, shopping or whatever, but the important thing is already in. Look at it the other way around, and that's when difficulties arise. When you treat an activity as something to be fitted in, you open up the possibility that it won't be. When you prioritise an activity – treat it is as something akin to eating and sleeping – you guarantee that it will be done.

You're playing psychological games with yourself here of course but you have time for everything if you prioritise in the right way. There are 24 hours in each day and night – you need perhaps half of one of those hours to fulfil all your exercise needs. There are *no* valid excuses for not having it already fitted in to your day.

Quick Decisions Can Have Long-term Implications.

Nobody 'respectable' ever had tattoos when I was young. You either had them as a result of teenage rebellion, through being a Hell's Angel, or because you'd got very drunk one night and woken up the next morning with some girl's name you'd never heard of, emblazoned on your buttocks.

But times have changed. Today, people of all ages and backgrounds have tattoos. It has become fashionable, and the styles and positions of tattoos are subject to fashion too. Where once you might have had an anchor on your forearm, now you're more likely to have some obscure oriental symbol across your lower back, or a Maori design across your shoulder. More recently, I've noticed script across the abdomen and down the side of the torso has become popular.

Would you go into a hairdressing salon and choose a hairstyle that you were going to keep for the rest of your life? Would you go into a clothes shop and pick a pair of trousers you were going to be sewn into and never be able to change? Of course you wouldn't, because fashions change and you want to be able to keep up with the trends of the day.

In 20 or 30 years' time, young kids will be laughing at the 'coloured-in' older generation and will be able to age them, not by their wrinkles, but by the design of their tattoos. What seems cool and cutting-edge now will seem tired, dated and old hat by the next generation. And the tattooed masses will be stuck with it… permanently branded by a particular era. Just like their anchor-wearing predecessors. The truth is that fashion is for the frivolous, disposable and temporary things in life. Tattoos are none of these things.

Getting a tattoo is just one irreversible decision that many young people enter into without much thought. There are many others. These decisions are usually regretted sooner rather than later. So give careful consideration to the timescale of the impact of any decisions you make and the availability of any viable and ethical escape routes from them. Will you still be living with the result of this decision in five, 10 or 20 years? Is there an easy way to retrace your steps if it doesn't work out as you'd hoped or the tattoo no longer appeals? If these are uncomfortable questions, perhaps it's time for a rethink.

Success Will Make You A Target.

So there we were, out for a power walk (okay stroll) on a lovely warm summer's evening, when the conversation turned to bird crap and the likelihood of being hit by it.

Now you might think this is an odd subject to be discussing in such circumstances, but that's because you don't walk with your 13-year-old daughter. If you did you would know that strange as the subject of conversation may appear, it is infinitely preferable to the usual topic that broadly falls into three basic themes.

1. What Jessica/Emily/Chloe said on Facebook today and why it was just SO unfair.

2. Why Mrs 'Whatchamacallit' is the worst teacher... ever.

3. Whether to wear the black or red top/coat/jeans/pyjamas for the next sleepover/party.

Anyway, back to the bird crap, which came as a welcome relief.

My daughter kicked things off by saying that cars are often covered in the stuff, but it's quite rare for people to get splattered. We quickly decided that cars are outside for more of the time, are often parked under trees, and are just a lot bigger (well, usually!) than people. We then turned to the question of why some people get 'hit' more than others. It was then that she expounded her theory: *"The narrower your shoulders, the less chance you're gonna get poohed on!"*

It's hard to argue with the logic of that, and I couldn't help thinking that it was a pretty accurate metaphor for life as well.

Much of what I'm writing about in this book is concerned with helping you to become a more successful person – to help you 'broaden your shoulders' and improve your lifestyle. I tend to focus on the positive aspects of that (of which there are many) but have thus far avoided the other side of the coin.

When you broaden your shoulders, you almost inevitably become more visible, and when you become more visible, you become a target. The broader your shoulders, the bigger target you become and the chances that you will take a direct hit at some point become depressingly high. Those dishing the dirt are motivated by a couple of thoughts – jealousy and greed. You have assets, resources, status or 'standing' and they want to either relieve you of those things or get their own hands on some of it.

So who are these dark forces that don't trouble you when you're part of the crowd, but start to smell blood as soon as they sense you're having some success? Well, in no particular order of either likelihood or severity, you can expect one or more of the following to start raining excrement down in your direction at some point:

- Friends and family
- HMRC and a bunch of other government departments
- Ex wives, husbands or partners
- Predatory lawyers
- Con artists
- Thieves and burglars
- Opportunist litigators
- The media
- Employees and former employees
- Neighbours
- Internet trolls
- Desperate entrepreneurs

I could go on.

As targets go, I'm not the biggest, but I've been poohed on by a number – but by no means all – of those sources, and fully expect a further dousing in the years to come. If I'd been broke and unsuccessful, none of this would have happened, but a great deal more good stuff wouldn't have happened either. There's a price to be paid for everything, and this is one of the prices we pay for success. So what can you do to protect yourself?

Well 'playing a straight bat', keeping your wits about you and keeping a low profile certainly help. But the latter isn't always possible, or desirable. The good things you have going on in your life may require that your profile is kept high, and why the heck should you work hard for success and then live like a hermit pauper anyway? What's the point in that? A little self-restraint though, and a situational sensitivity can definitely help. As with many things in life, forewarned is forearmed. Consider this your warning and your gratis trip to the ammo dump.

Now I know there are some people who will use this potentially negative aspect of success as an excuse for doing nothing – for maintaining their mediocrity. *"I don't want to become a target and so I'm going to just potter along in anonymity,"* they'll say. *"It's just not worth it."* Do you think I'm being harsh calling it an excuse?

Well there's a simple way to find out – ask those people (or yourself if it was your immediate reaction) whether they buy lottery tickets. If the answer is no, then I commend them for the choice they've made. But if the answer is yes, it isn't the crap that inevitably comes with wealth and success that they fear; it's the hard work that it can take to get there. And deep down they know the truth: despite becoming a target, being solvent and successful beats being poor and struggling every time. The only question is whether you're prepared to pay the price for being there.

Expensive Possessions Are Often A Burden.

I once heard Lord Sugar speaking at a charity lunch in London. He said that he used to own a yacht but he had sold it. The reason was, that the hassle far outweighed the pleasure. Every time he went on board, the captain would meet him with a list of problems – one of the engines wasn't working, the rudder was sticking or there was an expensive leak somewhere. He said that it took away the enjoyment of ownership and so he sold it.

I've never owned a yacht, but have owned enough 'toys' to recognise the problem. Fancy cars, for example, require expensive servicing, maintenance, parts and insurance. Run an old banger, and you have to worry about none of this. Nor do you have to worry where you're going to leave it and whether it's going to be damaged (or indeed still be there!) when you return. Even a luxury wristwatch needs expensive servicing, specialist insurance and when worn, there's a fear that it will be scratched or damaged in some way. No such fears when you have a £30 Seiko.

The bottom line is that whatever expensive possessions you have, they're probably going to be a source of cost, worry and hassle to you and, depending on your personality, these could easily outweigh any pleasure of ownership. So what do you do, if you have the wherewithal but don't want the hassle?

Well Lord Sugar indicated one viable solution at that lunch. Instead of owning a yacht he now charters one whenever he needs one. Maintenance, servicing, insurance and repairs are someone else's problem. For stuff you don't need or use all the time, rental seems a sensible option. And there's another big benefit too. You see with the exception of property, most high-ticket items depreciate, alarmingly. So not only are they a burden, but they also shed value too. Tying money up in a depreciating asset that is causing you sleepless nights makes little or no sense.

I fully realise you will pay absolutely no heed to any of this of course. If you are fortunate enough or skilled enough to accumulate enough spare cash to buy toys, that's what you will do, and find that I was right all along. Even though I won't be there, I am already taking great pleasure in saying: 'I told you so', at some date in the future!

You Have Fewer Friends Than You Think.

Ask people how many friends they have and you will find a strange paradox – as people get older the number of friends they claim to have falls. This has less to do with the truth of the situation than it has with the individual's awakening realisation of reality.

When you're young it's very easy to see drinking buddies, workmates and people, with whom you share a common interest, as friends. Some of these people will be friends, but at that moment in time, they might not have proved themselves to be so. It's human nature that we like to be seen to have a lot of friends (Facebook has done pretty well out of that!) But there's little sense in kidding yourself. When you get older, you have a lot less friends than you think.

Many of the people you call friends when young, are nothing of the sort. They are people who are happy to share your company when the going is good. You socialise together, play sports together, study together or work together. They will only prove themselves to be a friend in the true sense when things get tough – when you need them to provide help and support when things are not going well. This will require them to sacrifice their own time, money or effort to do something that will help or benefit you, but does nothing positive for them. In other words, they need to give something up to make your life better.

Older people claim to have fewer friends than younger ones because they have discovered, through experience, that the number of people prepared to sacrifice something for them is not a large one. Most people, by the age of thirty, realise that they can count the number of real friends they have on one hand – and usually have fingers left.

There's little you can do about this, other than be aware of it. Be alert to signs of genuine friendship and how they differ from those of good-time acquaintances or associates. And then nurture and cherish all the genuine friendships you have left. They are few and far between.

You Get To Choose Your Battles. So Choose Them Wisely!

Life offers daily opportunities to get involved in disputes, fights and battles. Someone says something we don't like, behaves in an unpleasant manner, appears to disrespect us, or says/does something else that makes us angry. It's an opportunity to go to war!

Most of the time they are just that though – opportunities, and like all opportunities we can either take them up or let them slide. Experience suggests that letting them slide is often the best approach.

Many battles are embarked upon to save face or self-esteem. It's done for ego purposes and little else. This is usually a mistake because the costs outweigh any potential benefits. At best a great deal of emotional energy is wasted to no good effect, and at worst there is an escalation in the dispute that results in a real problem that need never have arisen.

If you want to see this from the comfort of your own home, log on to virtually any Internet forum and watch perfect strangers get involved in battles and disputes over the most trivial of things. Someone says something vaguely controversial, someone else rises to it and within a few minutes they are hurling abuse at each other and threatening to beat each other senseless. In the real world, things tend to develop a little slower, but the principle is the same.

Think very carefully before engaging in any dispute. If a victory is likely to be pyrrhic or pointless, there is absolutely no sense or value in getting involved. Even the smallest dispute can escalate to an unimaginable level. Far better to avoid the battle, than find yourself in the midst of one that will not benefit you, regardless of whether you win or lose. Of course there are times we need to make a stand – when the result of not doing so could be seriously detrimental. However, these occasions are, thankfully, few and far between.

I'm not suggesting that you allow yourself to be pushed around or walked over, but I am suggesting you take a deep breath and ask yourself what significance does this battle hold? Am I just trying to bolster my ego or is there something more important at stake? What will happen if I say or do nothing and just walk away? What will I gain by achieving a win and what might the cost be?

When you answer these questions honestly, arguments, disputes and battles are things you can primarily watch from the sidelines.

School May Have Banished Winners And Losers. Life Has Not!

In their attempts to level out the playing field and blur the distinction between winners and losers, schools seem to have come a long way over the past couple of decades. Competitive sports have been sacrificed in favour of more collaborative physical activity, in which everyone can take part and there is no sense of one student prevailing over another. In academic matters, where a student is perceived to have an inherent weakness in a particular field or subject, every effort is made to give them additional assistance and help, which often culminates in them being given extra time to complete tests and examinations. All of this is done in the name of equality and fairness.

I'm not going to get into the rights and wrongs of this approach, other than to say that it doesn't appear to be the ideal preparation for later life. Schools may have attempted to eliminate competition, inequality and winners and losers, but the world certainly hasn't. Whichever field of endeavour you decide to enter, there will be competition. Some people will win and some will lose, and nobody is particularly concerned with making it 'fairer' for those who are likely to lose. They just want the best.

No matter whether it's competition for a job, a promotion, a place in a team or even a mate, the natural laws of the universe demand that the role goes to the person very best suited to it. Out in the real world, it's unlikely that your shortcomings will be taken account of. Fairness doesn't come into it. The universe demands that you compete with everyone else, and let the best man or woman, win.

What this means is that you need to nurture a mental attitude that recognises and accepts competition. Following on from that is an acceptance that nobody is about to level the playing field or make it easier for you, for any reason. If you want something, then you have to do everything in your power to compete for it. It's your responsibility to compete, and if you don't get what you want, then either you didn't work hard enough or it simply wasn't within your capabilities.

I hope this section doesn't come across as too harsh or uncaring – I suspect it does. My goal is to prepare you for the world as it is, not as I might like it to be. If I leave you waiting for someone to make things easier or 'fairer', then I will have given you the wrong impression of how the world really works.

Different Outcomes Require Different Actions.

This seems ridiculously obvious, but so many people seem to expect a different outcome from the same actions.

When looking for a new job, they continue to send out the same boring CV, despite the fact that it isn't winning interviews. If they're lucky enough to get an interview, they give the same responses to questions that they did at the last dozen unsuccessful interviews, hoping that this interviewer will respond better.

In business, they persist in advertising their products and services in broadly the same way and hope, that by some miracle, more people will start buying them. They use the same tired sales pitch and then complain because people are still showing them the door. They reduce their prices, hoping that it will have a better effect than when they tried the same thing last year.

In their personal lives, they walk straight into the same arguments, disputes and wrangles because they continue to do and say the same things that caused the trouble last time. They somehow hope that the other party will have changed their position and respond differently – but they haven't and they don't. They try to get people to do what they want, by doing what they've always done. And those people respond by doing what they've always done. The wrong thing!

There are rare exceptions, but by and large, if we continue to do the same things, we're going to get the same results. So if we're unhappy with the results we're getting in any aspect of our life, then we have to change what we're doing. Scientists know this for sure. Thousands of controlled experiments have etched it on their brains. In the uncontrolled environment of the outside world though, things are not quite so clear-cut or easy to comprehend, particularly where emotions come into play and random, unexpected variables can really throw a spanner in the works.

Unless for some massive dose of good fortune, doing what you've always done will get you what you've always got. If that's good enough for you, keep doing it. But if it isn't, you need to make changes.

If You'd Rather Be Lying On A Beach, You're On The Wrong Track.

Once I'd made some serious money, there was a question that started cropping up on a regular basis. It was couched in various terms, but the gist can be summed up as follows: *"Why the heck are you still working when you could be lying on a beach somewhere?"*

When someone first asked me that question many years ago, I was a bit taken aback. You see, it had never really occurred to me that 'doing nothing' was a desirable long-term strategy for anyone – no matter whether they have money or not. But when I got to thinking about it, and started playing back the conversations I've had over the years, I realised that there are a lot of people who think this way. Their goal is to acquire a pile of money and then metaphorically sit on top of it while soaking in the Sun's rays.

But here's what's interesting. This point of view is almost exclusively confined to people who are broke. Wealthy people rarely, if ever, think like this, and so there's a bit of a catch-22 paradox going on here. The people who can afford to lay on a beach all day don't want to do it, and the people who want to lay on a beach all day can't afford to do it. These two facts are not unconnected.

Most people, who have made enough cash to retire on, have a secret – the thing they did to make their money wasn't like work at all. Oh sure, it would have looked like work to anyone watching, but they enjoyed doing it. The fact that they found something they enjoyed doing was central to their success because it carried them through the difficult times that inevitably impact on any endeavour. It enabled them to put every last ounce of effort into making it a success. And they don't want to stop. Noel Coward explained it like this: *"Work is more fun than fun."*

Why would anyone want to stop working if it's fun, makes them a great deal of money and provides them with a far greater sense of achievement and self-worth than a life of idle luxury ever could? This is something that the 'Why aren't you lying on a beach?' merchants can never understand. You see their only experiences of work are negative ones. They're experiences are characterised by compulsion, restriction, scarcity and misery rather than voluntary action, freedom, abundance and excitement. Their concept of work is completely opposed to mine, so is it any wonder that they find it hard to understand why I might feel differently about it?

I think if you're reading this book, it's safe to assume that achieving financial success is part of your life plan. Want to know if your current job or business is likely to do it for you? You could do a lot worse than ask yourself this question: If £2 million landed in your bank account tomorrow, would you carry on doing what you're doing… or would you pack it in and head for the beach?

If you'd head straight for the beach (or whatever idle luxury means for you) then you're almost certainly in the wrong job or business. You're definitely not in a business or job that is going to give you the maximum chance of achieving your financial goals. If you're only doing it for the money, you're never going to be committed enough to achieve outstanding success.

So many people choose businesses and jobs because they believe it's where the money is, rather than deciding what they really want to do – and then going all out to become the very best at it. When you do that, the money finds you – rather than the other way around. It's so much easier having money chase you, than doing the chasing yourself into areas you don't really care for.

When that happens, you have the best of both worlds… the money and an enjoyable and absorbing way to make it. Every day becomes a game you play rather than boring work to be done. And the beach can look a pretty mundane alternative to that.

You Look Great Now!

As you look in the mirror and frown because you've just got a spot, your nose isn't quite the right shape or your hair doesn't look the way you'd like, I want you to understand something. In years to come you will look back on photographs of yourself today and be amazed how great you looked when you were young. There's a popular saying that you don't appreciate what you have until it's gone, and that's certainly the truth here. So many people gaze wistfully at old photographs of their younger self and wonder why they didn't have the confidence to grasp more opportunities – why they allowed false and negative feelings about their appearance to hold them back.

You have something that older people with more money, more experience, more skills and more power can never have – you have the unique beauty that comes with youth. And you have a choice. Either you can enjoy, embrace and capitalise upon it, or you can deny its existence, succumb to insecurity and set yourself up for a lifetime of 'if onlys' a couple of decades down the road.

Your Time Is Vital.

I don't mean this in a 'time is money' kind of way. This is much more important than that. You see the most precious thing you can give anyone else in your life is your time. Gifts or money are very poor substitutes that are quickly forgotten and often resented.

Your time and attention are what really matter. This holds true for all the important relationships in your life – as a child or grandchild, as a sibling, as a partner, as a friend and as a parent. If you want to keep your relationships healthy then it's vital that you invest time in them. Sadly this is one area where there are no shortcuts. You can't pay anyone to do this for you no matter how successful or wealthy you become. It's something only you can do.

Throughout your life, the pressure on your time will become intense. How well you manage the competing attention for each twenty-four hour day will be a massive determinant of the health of the key relationships in your life.

The World Doesn't Care About You.

The world, or certainly the collective of the people in it, doesn't really care about you and your wants, needs and aspirations. It has its own wants, needs and aspirations and is far more concerned about those. Its interest in you is confined to what value you can provide for it. This may sound harsh, but it's true and it has important implications for how you should best interact with the world around you if you want to give yourself the best chance of getting what you want.

US President John F Kennedy famously said in his inauguration speech in 1961: *"Ask not what your country can do for you; ask what you can do for your country."* He wasn't talking about personal success when he said it, but by replacing a couple of words in that quote, I think we get close to the secret of this with: ask not what the world can do for you, but ask what you can do for the world.

Other people – the world – don't want to hear about your wants and needs; they're really not interested. (As mentioned, their main focus is self-centred.) But when you talk to them in terms of their needs – about what they want rather than what you want – something magical happens; you automatically become one of the most agreeable and fascinating people they have ever met. Why? Because you are talking about the most important thing in the world to them – themselves. A simple thing to do you may think, however, most people are far too self-absorbed to do it.

And here's the really interesting thing – when you help people towards getting what they want, the likelihood is that they will help you get what you want. This may not happen immediately, or indeed directly, but it will happen. Start doing stuff for the world and the world will start doing stuff for you. But if you insist on the world listening to your requirements first, you will have a long, painful and ultimately fruitless, wait for satisfaction.

Making Enemies Is Madness.

Conflict in life is inevitable. We're all competing for scarce resources and it's impossible for everyone to get everything that they want. Two people want the same job, contract or house for example, so someone must lose out on the big prize. No matter whether the battle is over money, possessions, a job, some business, a relationship or just 'their own way', there is bound to be conflict to a greater or lesser extent. Your interests are often opposed to those of the people around you.

You want to win – of course you do – but those who pride themselves on a 'win-at-all-costs' attitude are deluding themselves if they think that this is a sensible long-term strategy. Yes, you can win individual battles with this approach, but the longer war often becomes increasingly problematic as a result. Why? Because you create a growing band of enemies who will be very keen to make your life more difficult further down the line, when they get the opportunity. And these opportunities arise far more often than you might imagine. As I said earlier when talking about burning bridges, paths have a habit of crossing.

It won't always be possible to avoid making enemies – you are, after all, relying on the goodwill of third parties – but there are certain things you can do to keep things under reasonable control.

Where possible, aim to reach win-win resolutions to negotiations or disputes. If you can find a way to satisfy both parties' needs, you can avoid any ill feeling. This isn't something that most people aim for, in fact, it often seems that they are more concerned with the other party losing than they are with their own victory. That's the kind of attitude that creates unnecessary enemies.

So a win-win resolution to any dispute should always be your preferred choice. If that isn't possible, there are still things you can do to minimise the chances of animosity giving rise to problems at a later date.

If it's clear that you are going to prevail, start looking for ways to allow your opponent to save face. That could be giving them something else that they want or making a minor concession. This may cost you something in the short term, but will often prove to be a solid long-term investment. If your opponent feels they have gained something out of the dispute – or at least that it looks to the world like they've gained something – then it's less likely that they will seek some kind of face-saving revenge or payback later. It's also far more likely that they will deal with you again.

Approach both victories and defeats with magnanimity, rather than the more usual reactions of gloating and resentment and you will go a long way to keeping your enemies to a minimum and a clear playing field out in front of you.

Pain and Discomfort Are Good!

As humans, it seems like we have a natural propensity to gravitate towards comfort in all things. We seek out warmth, freedom from hunger and other physical comfort of course, but it goes further than that. We seek out the psychological comfort too, the sort that can be found in the familiar, the safe and the unchallenging. We shy away from what we perceive to be dangerous, difficult and unknown. We shun what is uncomfortable. And yet it is precisely in discomfort that success is rooted.

There is no growth in comfort. Go to the gym and work within your known limits and you will not improve. Why would you? Your body is already capable of dealing with the challenges you're giving it. It has no reason to change. Your brain works in exactly the same way. Expose it to the same inputs, day in and day out, and nothing will change, but introduce it to new challenges, dangers and uncertainty and it will be forced to grow. This is, however, more difficult than it might appear, because comfort is… well, comfortable!

One way to start tackling this is to resolve to do something each day that scares you. There are few more certain ways of escaping your comfort zone than that. Now I'm not talking about 'playing chicken' on the M1, but rather the sort of things that will be beneficial to your targets and goals. This will mean different things to different people, but it could mean speaking in front of a group of people, telephoning prospective customers about a new business idea, asking for a promotion or rise, inviting that girl or boy on a date, running three miles more than you've run before or something else. You will know what this means for you.

The important thing is that you face up to, and embrace, discomfort. Why does a proposed course of action make you feel uncomfortable? Because it involves an uncertain outcome. But if you stay comfortable, you know exactly what the outcome will be – the same as you got before, or worse. You see, as others step out of their comfort zones they will start taking what was previously yours. Not only is there no growth in comfort, there is decline and reverse. Nothing stays the same. Standing still usually means moving backwards.

Determining The Worst Will Help You Do Your Best.

The default towards comfort is rooted in fear. While we're operating within our comfort zone we feel safe. We might not be getting or achieving everything we want, but at least we know what the outcome of our actions and activities will be, and we can live with it. But what exactly are we frightened of?

The interesting thing is that, for the most part, we never bother to rationalise any of this. We don't sit down and ask ourselves a couple of searching questions. *"What exactly am I afraid of here?"* And most importantly of all: *"What's the worst that can happen if I try to do this?"* When we do, we often realise that the worst that can happen isn't really that bad at all – back where we started and a little wiser for the experience. Perhaps a little embarrassment added in for good measure.

When I gave up work to start in business I realised that the worst that could happen would be that the business would fail and I'd have to get another job – just like I was already doing. Whenever I've had to make a big financial commitment or investment, I've calculated the worst-case scenario if it went wrong, and then decided accordingly. Every decision, big or small, becomes so much easier once the 'what's the worst thing that can happen?' question has been addressed.

Asking 'what's the worst that can happen?' will help push you out of your comfort zone and towards success. It will also help you identify genuinely risky endeavours, ones where the risk doesn't justify the potential reward and your comfort zone is the best place to be.

The Universe Repays Good Deeds.

I read a quote from legendary film actor Jack Lemmon, which perfectly encapsulates something that I've tried to act upon, and strongly recommend that you do too. He said that when anyone enjoys a degree of success in any field, they have a moral obligation to: *"send the elevator back down."* I think that's a great way of putting it, and an important message.

When people first achieve success, the natural inclination is to do just the opposite – to protect their position and jealously guard the knowledge, skills and information that got them to where they are. The feeling is that by sharing it with others, it's somehow diluted and diminished. My experience, like that of Jack Lemmon I'd imagine, is the opposite. Every time I've been in a position to *"send the elevator back down"* – and this book is one such opportunity – it has been repaid with a reward far in excess of the effort required to give that elevator button a bit of a push.

The reward isn't always received directly, or indeed in a way you might expect, but it comes all the same. It's just the way of the world I think – you do something to help, and you're rewarded for it. How that reward comes will depend on the business, field or circumstances you're in, but come, it will.

Now here's something you might not have considered; in some areas of your life, you're already on one of the 'upper floors'. Indeed, you don't even need to be battling with vertigo for this to apply to you. If you're anywhere above the basement, there are people you can send the elevator down for. You have it in your power to send the elevator back down for someone. It could be family, friends or people you don't even know yet.

Give some thought to the areas of your life in which you're riding high and admiring the view… and what you can do to speed others' ascent to the same heights. It feels good to do, and in the long run, it will almost certainly pay dividends.

Technology Is Just A Tool.

Technology has never moved faster, and digital-based technology is at the forefront of this tsunami. Hardly a day goes by without the appearance of some new device, software, website or app, to supposedly help us go about our business quicker, cheaper or better – or all of those things. These are exciting times, but they're also frightening ones. And the main fear is this; that we're getting left behind.

This fear is excellent news for the digital industry, because we spend a small fortune on new systems, hardware and software to make ourselves feel better... and then wonder what to do with it when we get it home, or back to the office. To paraphrase Winston Churchill: never has so little been done by so many, with so much! Most computer systems and software packages are chronically under-utilised, and yet fear makes us buy more and more.

It's like buying a ten-ton truck and then only using it to fetch the shopping from Sainsbury's! There's more spare capacity than you could ever use, and it's not even the best tool for the job.

In my humble little business we process an average of 700 individual orders each day – some days it can be as many as 2,000. And yet it's all done on 15-year-old software. In computer terms that's prehistoric. (So-called experts look at what we use and laugh.) But here's the interesting thing... it works. The job gets done, and not one of these experts has been able to put forward an alternative that, on close examination, provides measurable benefits in excess of the inevitable problems and disruption that a change would cause.

You see, the experts are in love with the technology and they're in awe of what it can do. But these are just features. What matters most is how we can use the technology to achieve something that's important to us. Some people will always immerse themselves in the technology itself, rather than the real and tangible profit-making benefits it can bring. They're the sort of people who buy a hi-fi system with 1001 buttons, knobs and dials and spend hours painstakingly adjusting them... before playing their new death metal CD. It's a counterproductive and time-wasting approach.

For the most part, it seems that software and hardware advances create solutions to problems that simply don't exist, and are neither important to us nor central to our success. If you've got a pile of crap to shift you won't do it any better or quicker with a silver-plated shovel!

Look carefully at the problems you want your technology to solve. If you have piles of the unmentionable to deal with, think very carefully about whether that new shovel (yes, I know it has got some nice engraving on the handle) is really worth the additional investment. Will it pay for itself, or would your old shovel do the job just as well?

Next, take a fresh look at the tools you already have – your hardware and software. I know that when you do you'll discover features and applications that you didn't know were there.

Technology is a tool. Nothing more, nothing less. Its only value is in what it can do for you and you will only unlock that potential by exploring it fully and then learning how to extract the maximum value. Look at each apparent development in these simple, clinical terms and you'll save yourself a lot of time, a great deal of money and a whole barrel-load of stress.

Selling Your Labour Is A Sure Route To Mediocrity.

Most of us start out by selling our labour – it's called a job, but as a long-term strategy for getting through life as a 'free' man or woman, it's a questionable approach at best. I'll put this as clearly as I can – if financial freedom is important to you, you will need to break the link between hours worked and money earned as quickly as possible.

To be financially free requires you to work because you choose to do so not because you have to. To do that, you have to accumulate sufficient assets to generate a passive income large enough to sustain yourself – and any dependants – and that's next to impossible if you're paid a salary or paid by the hour. Your earnings will always be limited by the pay scales of employers and the restraints imposed by the number of hours you can physically work in a day, week and year.

There are exceptions of course – Premiership footballers, directors of major organisations, stock market traders, TV presenters and the like – but these aren't jobs that are open to most of us. And the ones that are (even the 'good' ones) don't pay nearly well enough to flip us over from working because we have to, to working because we want to.

Become a doctor, a head teacher, a lawyer, a dentist, an accountant, a company director or an architect and you'll be comfortable... but accumulate enough money to make work a matter of choice rather than necessity? It's unlikely. No, the only sure-fire way to do that is to write your own pay cheque – to sever the relationship between the number of hours you work and the amount of money you are paid. And the only time-tested and proven way to do this is to run your own business or enterprise.

Now none of this may matter to you. You may be happy and content to work through necessity right up to whatever the retirement age is by the time you get there (probably about 85 if the current trend continues!) There's nothing wrong with that; it's what most people do. But I want you to be very clear about what you're signing up for and what you need to do if you want something different for yourself.

Not Knowing What You Want To Do Is Normal.

There's no getting away from it – what you do for a living tends to define you, and for that reason, it's important. I didn't have the first idea what I wanted to do when I was young – and to a certain extent, nothing has changed – but it didn't seem to matter that much. But the world has moved on, and the pressure to have some kind of plan, grows evermore intense. Don't worry; it is just the old folk trying to make life hard for you. You don't need a definite plan – not yet anyway.

Unless you're one of the rare souls with a genuine calling towards something, or a heartfelt commitment, being uncertain (or having no idea at all) is perfectly normal. In the really old days, people had little choice. You were born into a particular background or family and there was no decision to make. You were going to be a farmer, a miner, a domestic servant or whatever everyone else did. But once a world of opportunities was opened up to everyone, widespread uncertainty and indecision became more prevalent. So what do you do?

All you can do, in practical terms, is keep investigating and experimenting with different ideas and career paths, while keeping your options as open as possible. What does this mean? Well if you drop the study of maths and sciences, for example, you rule out a huge swathe of career possibilities straight away. Drop the study of social sciences and it places virtually no limitation on what you might do in the future. A mathematician can become a lawyer or a journalist. A sociologist can also become a lawyer or a journalist, but can't become a doctor or an engineer.

Maths and sciences aren't for everyone though, and neither are the subject-specific careers to which they lead. There's little point in toiling with these subjects if you know for sure that none of the areas where they are needed, are for you. So spend a little time at first deciding which doors you want to leave open, rather than which one you ultimately want to pass through – start with what you don't want to do and work backwards. You'll get there sooner or later. Everyone does. No rush.

Negative People Have
No Place In Your Life.

There are two groups of people in your life right now. One group is characterised by giving and sharing, the other by taking. One group is encouraging and supportive; the other is critical and subversive. One group wants you to succeed; the other is waiting for you to fail. One group wants you to grow and prosper, the other group is afraid you'll leave them behind. One group leaves you enthused and motivated; the other leaves you deflated and dejected. Both groups claim to have your best interest at heart, but only one really does. One group has a positive impact on your life; the other has a negative one.

If you're to make the most of your life, it's vital that you keep the 'positives' close by and jettison the 'negatives'. You know who they are. They're the ones who always pour cold water on your ideas, the ones who criticise you, the ones who dump their problems at your door but have no interest in yours, the ones who leave you feeling angry or sad, the ones who you spend time with and end up feeling worse than you did before. They claim to be your friends, but they are nothing of the sort. They are not givers. They are not sharers. They are takers.

It may seem harsh to suggest that you banish these people from your life, but you must. The road is tough enough without carrying passengers who are consciously or subconsciously intent on sabotaging your chances of reaching your destination. Don't make the mistake of thinking they are going through a difficult time, or that they will change. This is how they are. They won't change. If anything, they will get worse.

You need partners on the journey who will truly support and encourage you. For the most part, these will be people intent on taking a similar journey – positive and enthusiastic people who you can support – and be supported by – in a mutually beneficial relationship. They are like-minded people who will work with you – not against you. They are real friends, rather than friends in name only. They will help you get to where you want to be, but only if you cast aside the 'dead wood' first.

Everyone Feels Fear.

You know all those fearless, confident people you're in awe of – the ones who seem to breeze through life, comfortable and in total control of their careers, social interactions and relationships? It's an act. Just as you put on a 'face' for the outside world that is at odds with what you're really feeling inside, so do they. They feel fear, just like you do, but they have learned to mask, control and channel it better than you have. Perhaps they have had more time to do it, or been fortunate enough to find a mentor or teacher to help them, but you can be sure that what you're witnessing is the control of fear rather than the absence of it.

Many people beat themselves up because they feel they are somehow weaker, more fearful and more scared than those around them. This is rarely true. It's just that those people have learned or developed systems for dealing with fear.

Fear is impossible to banish altogether, although exposure to the things and situations that engender fear will certainly help you to deal with it better. When you face up to your fear and nothing terrible happens, the fear is certain to diminish.

So treat fear as you would any challenge – something to be tackled and overcome rather than something to be avoided. You can be sure that those you admire for their courage and confidence have done precisely that.

There Is Only One Kind Of Secret.

This is so simple and blatantly obvious. However, few people seem to grasp the significance of it, and suffer all manner of pain and humiliation as a result. If it's important that you keep something confidential, tell nobody. Not your best friend, not your brother, not your parent, not your boyfriend or girlfriend. Nobody at all. Is that unequivocal enough for you?

The term 'sharing a secret' is an oxymoron. The moment you 'share' what was previously only a piece of information, it ceases to be a secret. You lose control of it for good. Its fate passes into the hands of others – people who you may believe you can trust with it – but you probably can't. How many times have you been told something in confidence by someone, who has also been told it in confidence, and who then had the temerity to swear you to secrecy? There are people who can be trusted to pass your secret no further, but it will be purely luck that determines whether they happen to be in your immediate circle. And who wants to rely on luck for something so important?

Now I'm not suggesting for one moment that you should live your life under a cloak of secrecy, revealing nothing to the people around you. But what I am suggesting is that you give very careful consideration to what you do reveal. Are you comfortable with the world knowing what you're about to 'share' – or at least the part of it that has an impact on you? If not, then you should tell nobody. It is simple as that.

Quality Is King.

I have to admit that for reasons that are not a total mystery to me, I have developed something of a reputation as a cheapskate. It's not as though I haven't spent a great deal of money over the years – much to the enrichment of hordes of dealers in expensive cars, wristwatches and antiques – but I do like to find a bargain. And that can result in trouble.

I have often found myself buying stuff because it's in the sale or a 'bargain' rather than because it's something I really want and need. Like the character in the Monty Python piston engine sketch – Google is your friend here – I have accumulated numerous strange items for no better reason than they were 'a bargain'. (I've even bought clothing that's the wrong size, simply because it was a little bit cheaper!) And I've ignored better-quality items that I could very comfortably afford because they were more expensive.

The Gucci family slogan used to be: *"Quality is remembered long after the price has been forgotten."* Now you might argue that they have a vested interest, but it's hard to argue, especially when it's put slightly differently: you live with poor quality long after any saving has been forgotten.

The old adage of *"buy cheap, buy twice"* carries a lot of truth. Buying cheaply is often a false economy that results in buying twice – and sometimes three and four times. Add in time-consuming trips to the returns department, inconvenience when things break or break down, and good old-fashioned psychological disappointment and my buy cheap habit looks all the more ridiculous.

It's taken me an awful lot of years to get to the point of accepting this, (and like a struggling alcoholic, I still have occasional lapses) but you have the opportunity to save yourself a whole boatload of time, heartache and money by taking it on board now.

Being Interesting Is Easy.

One of the greatest insults you can bestow upon anyone is to label them 'boring', and it's for that reason that most of us make an effort to ensure that the label isn't attached to us. Unfortunately, the effort is often misguided and misdirected. Whenever I hear of someone who is *"the life and soul of the party"*, *"larger than life"* or *"bubbly"* a little part of me dies, and I suspect it's the same for you. And yet, this is precisely the kind of persona that many of us try to present in order to appear interesting and stave off the 'boring' tag.

Being interesting isn't about being loud and gregarious. Fine if that's your natural personality but pointless and tiresome if it isn't. Nor is it about having dozens of stories to tell about your exploits, achievements, possessions or influential friends and family. The people around you may give the impression that these things impress them but the truth is that they don't. Being truly interesting is much simpler than any of that, and you don't need to have a mass of experiences, achievements and stories to do it. You see the people you want to make a favourable impression upon already have those and they can't wait to tell someone!

When you stop trying to be interesting, and focus instead on being interested, magical things happen. The people you're interacting with, in both business and social situations, will find you engaging company, even if you say very little. If they stopped to think about it for a moment, they'd find it difficult to explain why. The reason though is very simple; you've given them the opportunity to talk about their favourite subject in the whole world – themselves!

So how do you do this in practice? It's not difficult and certainly a great deal easier than trying to be something that you're not. You'll need to use words and phrasing that come naturally to you, but it involves little more than asking open questions, expressing interest in the answers you receive and then inviting the other person to expand on what they just told you – showing genuine interest, in other words. I've yet to meet a single person who is bored by someone who allows them to talk about themselves and then pays them the compliment of expressing interest in what they've just heard. On the other hand, I've met many people who have been on the point of exasperation in the company of someone whose idea of social discourse is to talk incessantly about their own exploits, achievements and contacts.

The key to being interesting is being interested, and an added bonus is that you may actually get to learn something. It's rare that you'll learn anything if you are talking.

You Can Permanently Dump Any Negative Habit In 21 Days Or Less.

Well here we are towards the end of the book, but at the start of yet another new year. What do you mean: *"It's not the start of a new year?"* Of course it is. Every day is the start of a new year. It might not be January 1st, but what the heck does that matter? It's just an arbitrary date – and terrible to use as a starting point for a fresh start.

Don't even think about making regular New Year's resolutions come January. They are a complete waste of time and effort... something for losers to do to kid themselves that they might make a difference to their existence in the following 12 months. By January 10th, everything has fallen apart leaving them to slump back into their comfy chair until the 'next big effort' in 12 months' time.

January 1st is just another day. There are at least 365 opportunities to make a fresh start this year, and none is better than any other. And there's another good reason for ignoring the traditional New Year's resolution game. Attempt to make too many changes at one time and – even you...yes you with the nerves of steel and fiery determination – will find it almost impossible to stick to all of them. And once you've failed, the negative memory will make it even harder for you to succeed next time.

We've covered a lot of ideas and potential changes in this book, and I hope you're keen to adopt at least some of them. What you need though is a framework for making a series of staged changes throughout the year... starting today! Put this plan to work – it will take some self-discipline – and you will make more positive changes to your life in the next 12 months than you have made in your entire life. The end result will be, literally, life-changing.

Proper Scientific-type People (PSTPs for short) have looked into this and found something pretty exciting. It takes an average of three weeks – just 21 days – to change a permanent habit. That may mean either eliminating a negative habit or forming a positive one. The key to changing a habit permanently is repetition. To make a habit or behaviour change stick you need to repeat it every day, without fail, for around three weeks. After that it becomes part of you. You have re-programmed yourself, if you like.

Now, if you tried to change several habits at once in this way, it simply wouldn't work. Most of us don't have the self-discipline to carry it through. But tackled systematically – one at a time – anyone can make these changes.

What? You don't find this exciting? It's too slow for you? Not a quick enough 'fix'? Well, think about it this way. Carry out the plan rigorously, and completely, and by the time the clock reaches midnight one year from today, you will have made 17 major habit changes.

The first stage in this process is deciding what your goals are, and then deciding which habit(s) you'll need to change to maximise your chances of reaching them. So the goal of improving your appearance and health may cause you to target habit changes in the areas of smoking, exercise, diet, grooming and alcohol intake. The goal of increasing your income may lead you towards habit changes in the areas of education, training, research, work rate, hours worked, interpersonal skills... and so it goes on.

Let's take a simple example. Your goal is to increase your income, and to do that, you feel you would benefit from working an extra hour each day: a reasonable assumption. An extra hour each working day equates to an extra 30 working days in a year. Where do you get the extra hour? How about sleeping time?

Your first habit goal is therefore to get up one hour earlier each day. To make the system work, you simply carry out the desired action every day for three weeks. Don't think beyond that three-week period at this stage. Just view it as something you're going to do for 21 days. That's all. At the end of that time the new habit will almost certainly be formed and will have become an integral part of the way you live your life. Now you can move on to your next task, and the next...

This is a deceptively powerful technique. Can you even begin to imagine the changes in your life if you use each of the three-week periods between now and this time next year, to make 17 positive and permanent habit changes? Can you conceive how much you'll have improved your chances of reaching your goals once you've done it? Just three weeks from today you can have broken your most self-destructive habit, or formed a new positive habit that will help catapult you towards your goals. But you have to start, and you have to start today.

And that's the difficult part. Because taking action, rather than thinking about it as a nice idea, is a habit in itself. And it's the first good habit you'll need to form before you can make this work for you. So what will you change in the next 21 days, and the next 12 months? Take positive action and the answer is everything you choose. Sit back and wait however, and the answer will be nothing.

In Closing.

It's always easy, when reading a book like this, to feel that someone who claims they have all the answers is lecturing you. I hope it hasn't come across like that because nothing could be further from the truth.

When I was in my teens, the ideas and approaches I've tried to get over to you in this book were totally alien to me. My background was such that this sort of thing just wasn't on my radar at all, and I can't tell you how many mistakes I've made and dead ends I've encountered as a result. I've learned and improved, and had a fair degree of success, but the job took a long time and is far from over. It never will be. If this were the finished article, I'd be asking for my money back!

Much of what I've written here was as much for me as it was for you. It served as a valuable reminder of things I knew, but for whatever reason, had either put to the back of my mind or stopped acting upon. And I hope, in time, it will do the same for you. You see, you can neither hope to internalise and implement 99 ideas from a single reading nor, as we've just seen, can you make multiple critical changes at the same time.

Some of the material here will have struck a chord with you straight away. You may even have started thinking and acting differently already. Other things, you will be less certain about – sceptical even. It will take time for you to fully appreciate them. And others won't seem relevant to you at all at the moment. It's for these reasons, that I'd urge you to re-read and revisit the book several times. The words won't change, but the person reading them will. As you experience new things and change accordingly, what makes little sense today could be a huge 'Aha!' moment a week, a month or a year from now. Each revisit should give you a fresh perspective.

I'd like this book to be the beginning of a relationship between us, not the end. Let me know what you thought of it. Are there any ideas, rules or strategies you think I've missed? Is there further information you'd like? Don't hesitate to get in touch and let me know. My contact details are below and I really would like to hear from you.

So we come to the end and I've saved the most critical factor until last. I know that what's written here can dramatically and rapidly change the path of your life for the better. It can make you wealthier, healthier and happier, with stronger and more fulfilling relationships with everyone around you. But it will only do that if you let it. Nothing happens by reading, but anything can happen by taking positive and enthusiastic action with what you've read. I really hope you will do that.

Good luck, and I look forward to hearing from you.

John Harrison

Email: John@streetwisepublications.co.uk
Website: www.streetwisejohn.com

Mailing Address:
John Harrison, c/o Eden House, Genesis Park, Sheffield Road, Rotherham, S60 1DX.

Bonus Chapter
– From *'Man Sets Fire To Friends Head*
– *The Least Worst Of John Harrison'*.

The Birthday Party.

There may be worse places for a grown man to spend two hours on a Sunday afternoon in February. But as I sat in a Wacky Warehouse last weekend, I couldn't readily bring one to mind.

Just in case you're mercifully free of offspring, and don't know what a Wacky Warehouse is, it's a kind of padded cell tagged on to the end of an awful pub, cunningly disguised as an indoor children's' adventure playground.

My daughter was there for yet another birthday party, and through a process which I still don't fully understand, I was somehow conned into accompanying her...a role which basically involves stopping her either killing or being killed. Why can't they play nicely?

To be honest, I didn't think it would be too bad. I had visions of all these sexy young mums desperate to latch on to the only bit of male company around...no matter how ragged around the edges that male company might be.

Then they'd go back and tell my wife how lucky she was to be married to a charming, good looking, sensitive bloke like me. And she'd get all jealous and cross and vow never to let me go to one of these parties ever again. Perfect!

But it wasn't to be.

All the 'party mums' had dressed for warmth, (I can only assume they didn't know I was coming) and were more interested in discussing the price of children's' shoes, than any razor sharp repartee I might be able to bring to the table. If I didn't know better, I'd swear none of them were even remotely interested in me at all

Anyway, I was left to idly scan the rest of the people in the room, and made a shocking discovery.. By an amazing coincidence, our visit to the Wacky Warehouse appeared to have coincided with a... Dysfunctional Family and Scumbag Convention.

That was the only explanation I could come up with for the human flotsam and jetsam before me...either that or the fact that the Wacky Warehouse is on the 'Shop Lifter Special' bus route from the local Dumpsville to a large retail park. I was starting to despair.

If the 'party mums' were dressed for warmth, the 'convention mums' seemed to be dressed for solicitation. Their mode of dress seemed to be something of a uniform...About half an acre of chalk white flab and stretch marks, exposed between cropped top and low slung trousers...punctuated with a gold belly-button stud. Like putting a cherry on a turd.

I was just wondering why these women would choose to display and highlight their worst feature, when one of the 'convention' walked past me and bent down to pick up her toddler, (who was, of course, called Britney, and for some reason, already had pierced ears at 18 months) and I realised the horrific truth...The belly wasn't the worst!

Two giant love handles spilled over her 3-sizes-too-small trousers...like those bolster cushions you get on the end of sofa. And protruding from 4 inches of exposed buttock cleavage, was clear evidence of a black lacy thong.

It was a scary sight, and one which reminded me of a story I heard recently about an old man who said that in his day, you used to have to move a woman's underwear to get to her arse...but now you have to move a woman's arse to get to her underwear!   I think you'd have needed a crow bar, a torch and maybe even a mining licence, before attempting to extricate this particular lady's underwear from its hiding place.

I was just contemplating the logistics of such an operation when the first of many wailing children came to the table.

First it was Georgina who was distraught because William had jumped on her. She didn't seem particularly comforted by my *"that's boys for you"* comment, by way of sympathy. Don't think I'm cut out for this child caring lark.

Next up was Millie, equally distraught because one of the other children had thrown up in the ball pool. Have you ever considered the implications of someone vomiting jelly and ice cream in a ball pool? Neither had I, but they're not nice, I can assure you.

And then came Stacey...*"a big boy is swearing at us and using a very naughty word"* she said. Everyone resisted the temptation to ask exactly what the word was, and a member of staff was despatched into the padded cell...sorry, play area...to drag out the offender.

She returned with an overweight, sweaty eight year old wearing a replica football shirt. His Dad was soon on the scene... 5'6" with bleached blond hair, arms full of tattoos, and wearing a grubby T shirt with 'FCUK YOU' printed on it in triplicate...just in case you missed it the first time.

*"Stop using f***ing language in front of t' little 'uns"* he said, suggesting that he didn't have an issue with his use of bad language per se...but rather the use of it in front of children whose language skills were not sufficiently developed to copy it properly.

"I didn't say owt", said the lad. *"Well you'd better f***ing not,"* said his dad, *"or you're f***ing going home."*

I was sorely tempted to discuss my views on breeding licences with him, but looked at his face and saw the scars of a dozen similar discussions.

I took the view that getting arrested for brawling in a Wacky Warehouse was going to look very bad on my CV, and even worse to my daughter. And while all this was going on, she was mercifully unaware of any of it...or was at least turning a blind eye, because the last thing she wanted was to go home.

And that's the point.

You see, no matter how much I hated the Wacky Warehouse experience, she loved it, and so did her friends. And I have to be honest...So did the Dysfunctional Family and Scumbag Convention!

If it wasn't for the Wacky Warehouse, none of those people would have been in that pub at 3 o'clock on a Sunday afternoon, and they wouldn't have been spending money on food and drink in there either. Fact is, in modern Britain, where the kids want to go, the parents are happy to follow and spend money.

It wasn't like that when I was growing up. Back then, as a kid, you were sort of an appendage. You were around but you had to fall in with what your parents were doing. It never occurred to them that they might organise some (or indeed any) of their life around you. You had little or no say in what you did as a family, or where you went, and as a consequence, how the family money was spent.

But now it's different. Whether you agree with it or not, there's no doubt that in many (if not most) families, the children either directly or indirectly have a big influence on how, when and where money is spent.

And this can happen in unexpected areas.

Most of the car dealerships I've been to recently now have facilities for children. Some have a mini crèche complete with toys and games...others have sweets, drinks and colouring books available, others have videos showing cartoons, or games machines.

Why?.

Because the owners know that little Johnny and Johnetta rule the roost, and if the little darlings get bored, then their parents won't stay. And if they don't stay, they won't buy a car. Simple.

I've seen exactly the same facilities provided in a number of retail outlets, where the purchase process is likely to be a lengthy one...kitchen companies, bathroom suppliers, furniture shops...and so on.

So, by way of compensating you for enduring my catharsis over Sunday afternoon, I'd like to leave you with three questions to ponder, the answers to which could make you a huge pile of money in the coming months:

1. Is there some child-friendly facility you could add to your business which would attract children...bringing their parents with them who might spend money on your primary product or service? That's what Wacky Warehouse is all about.

2. Is there some child friendly facility you could add to your business which will occupy your potential customers' children when they come to your business, and reduce the chances of 'Modern Child' losing you a sale? That's what the car dealers and high ticket retailers do.

3. Is there some way you can 'win over' your potential customers' children in a way which will cause those children to champion your cause with their parents? I'm talking bribery here!

On that last point, one simple idea might be to get hold of your customers' children's' birthdays, and make sure they receive a card and small present from the business.

Kids may not have a great deal of spending power, but they do have a great deal of influence over how, when and with whom, family money is spent. You might not like the little darlings...you may have spent your adult life studiously avoiding them...but if you ignore them, you're ignoring a powerful money making opportunity. Your competitors might not be making the same mistake.

Footnote:

When I eventually escaped from The Wacky Warehouse after 2 hours of hell, someone from The Dysfunctional Family and Scumbag Convention had backed their heap of scrap into my car. And I thought the day couldn't get any worse.

Extracted from *Man Sets Fire To Friends Head – The Least Worst Of John Harrison* ISBN 978-0-9557435-4-2 Published By Streetwise Publications, Eden House, Genesis Park, Sheffield Road, Rotherham S60 1DX. Tel 01709 820033 www.streetwisepublications.co.uk

A Message From The
Desk Of John Harrison...

Dear Reader,

I've always thought that putting together a 'best of' book is a bit big-headed to say the least, and in my case, not particularly honest.. Asking people to choose their favourite articles and chapters from my various books, newsletters and blogs is a bit like asking them to choose their favourite tropical disease. They'd rather avoid them all, but if pushed to make a decision, would pick the ones which are least likely to kill them, or leave any lasting damage.

It was with that thought in mind that I chose the subtitle of my book, Man Sets Fire To Friends Head....*the least worst of John Harrison*. The title itself comes from a hilarious local newspaper article which forms the basis of one of the more entertaining chapters. Who says you can't make a silk purse from a sows ear?

Other Chapters Include:

- How Getting The Sack Made Me Rich
- Pro-Celebrity Boxing
- John's Bedroom Secrets
- Film Star For A Day
- Harrison And The Saga Louts
- Roger Mellie Lives
- Wrestling Lessons
- No More Hygienically Challenged Dwarfs
- What The Fcuk
- CU2Moz...You Idiot
- Embarrassing Bodies
- Alcatraz, Achilles And How I Discovered The Secret Of Making A Great Deal Of Money

As I re-read that list I'm conscious of the fact that it may appear to the untrained eye, to be a collection of frivolous nonsense. Don't be fooled – please! I chose these chapters because they're the pieces that got the most reaction from readers. I'll have to admit that some of that reaction was outrage and fury, but mixed in there has been a fair sprinkling of genuine gratitude.

Some chapters made people think, some made them laugh, and then there are others that made them a great deal of money. Just the other day I received a letter from a guy who had raked in over £10 million using one of my ideas. You've no idea what sort of mixed emotions a letter like that can bring!

Anyway, people seemed to like this stuff on the whole. Here's what they said:

"Very Funny and an inspiration."
Barry Gold

"Well written and a laugh a minute."
Brendan McEvoy

"I can't remember when I enjoyed reading a book so much."
John Abbiss

"Great stuff John. I'm reading your book but doing the opposite of speed reading. I don't want to get to the end."
Robert Carter

"A brilliant book. "So true to life that it had me in stitches at times." "Very amusing and very astute."
Thomas Walden

"I thoroughly enjoyed it. The light-hearted humour along with the serious aspects made compulsive reading."
Stuart Warrilow.

I've included a copy of The Birthday Party chapter above, to give you a flavour of what you can expect. If you don't like that, you probably won't much care for the rest of it. In fact you're probably going to hate it if you're a stickler for political correctness or have a low tolerance threshold for jokes which might most charitably be called 'borderline'.

For everyone else though, I genuinely think you'll have a good time with it and maybe learn a thing or two. *Man Sets Fire To Friends Head – The Least Worst Of John Harrison* normally sells for £19.95, but as a buyer of *'Why Didn't They Tell Me?'* you can get hold of a copy for just ten pounds. Yes, just £10.

If you'd like a copy, give our customer hotline a call on either 01709 820033 or 01709 361819 at any time. Be sure to mention, 'Why Didn't They Tell Me' so you get the £10 deal.

Look forward to hearing from you soon.

Best Wishes,

John Harrison

P.S. Whether you want a copy of the book or not, don't forget you can contact me personally at any time at:

John@streetwisepublications.co.uk